Ten
Years
to
Midnight

Ten Years to Midnight

Four Urgent Global Crises and Their Strategic Solutions

Blair H. Sheppard

with Susannah Anfield, Ceri-Ann Droog, Alexis Jenkins, Thomas Minet, Jeffrey Rothfeder, and Daria Zarubina

Berrett–Koehler Publishers, Inc

Berrett-Koehler Publishers, Inc.
1333 Broadway, Suite 1000
Oakland, CA 94612-1921
Tel: (510) 817-2277 / Fax: (510) 817-2278
www.bkconnection.com

ORDERING INFORMATION

QUANTITY SALES. Special discounts are available on quantity purchases by corporations, associations, and others. For details, contact the Special Sales Department at the Berrett-Koehler address above.
INDIVIDUAL SALES. Berrett-Koehler publications are available through most bookstores. They can also be ordered directly from Berrett-Koehler: Tel: (800) 929-2929; Fax: (802) 864-7626; www.bkconnection.com.
ORDERS FOR COLLEGE TEXTBOOK/COURSE ADOPTION USE. Please contact Berrett-Koehler: Tel: (800) 929-2929; Fax: (802) 864-7626.

Distributed to the US trade and internationally by Penguin Random House Publisher Services.
Berrett-Koehler and the BK logo are registered trademarks of Berrett-Koehler Publishers, Inc.

Printed in Canada.

Berrett-Koehler books are printed on long-lasting acid-free paper. When it is available, we choose paper that has been manufactured by environmentally responsible processes. These may include using trees grown in sustainable forests, incorporating recycled paper, minimizing chlorine in bleaching, or recycling the energy produced at the paper mill.

Library of Congress Cataloging-in-Publication Data
  Names: Sheppard, Blair H., author.
  Title: Ten years to midnight : four urgent global crises and their strategic solutions / Blair H. Sheppard; with Susannah Anfield, Ceri-Ann Droog, Alexis Jenkins, Thomas Minet, Jeffrey Rothfeder, and Daria Zarubina.
  Description: Oakland, CA : Berrett-Koehler Publishers, [2020] | Includes bibliographical references and index.
  Identifiers: LCCN 2020008986 | ISBN 9781523088744 (hardcover) | ISBN 9781523088751 (pdf) | ISBN 9781523088768 (epub)
  Subjects: LCSH: Globalization--Economic aspects. | Globalization—Environmental aspects. | Leadership. | Political leadership.
  Classification: LCC HF1365 .S49 2020 | DDC 306.3—dc23
  LC record available at https://lccn.loc.gov/2020008986

First Edition

28 27 26 25 24 23 22 21 20 || 10 9 8 7 6 5 4

Book producer: BookMatters; Text designer: BookMatters; Cover designer: Jenny Forrest (PwC); Copyeditor: Amy Smith Bell; Proofer: Anne Smith; Indexer: Leonard Rosenbaum

To the woman who has been my companion through all of the experiences that shaped this book and whose patience made it possible, my wife, Martha.

CONTENTS

PREFACE

As I think about reading a book and how I want to consume it, I begin with four basic questions. Where did it come from—do I trust its origins? Who is it meant for—is it relevant to me? What are the intentions of the author(s)—do I care about what they are writing about? And what should I expect of the book—will I enjoy reading it? Assuming that at least a few of you think the same way, it is worth addressing these four questions as a way of helping to prepare you for what you are about to read.

This book has two origins. A first set of ideas was created with the other authors by a process of global discovery and expanded through an exhaustive look at the issues in sixteen particular countries. In some ways the joint creation of these ideas enabled not only the team listed on the front cover but also the host of PricewaterhouseCoopers (PwC) colleagues to better understand the evidence behind the worries at the heart of this book. A second set of ideas emerged from my own personal experience over four phases of my career. Working backward, these experiences include my time as the global head of strategy and leadership at PwC, a role that allows the sort of global access and perspective essential to the book's central claim that all of us share very similar worries; my time as dean of Fuqua School of Business at Duke University, during which I had the opportunity to discover the challenges of institutional change at a very personal level and the great fortune to identify the opportunity and negotiate the basic agreement for the founding of a campus for Duke in Kunshan, China; my experience as founder and CEO of Duke Corporate Education, the world's first truly global executive education business, during which I developed both an appreciation of the globalization, technology, and simple measures firsthand and honed my thinking on leadership and change; and finally, my years as a professor, during which the basic ideas of organization and society that served me throughout my career were first fully formed.

This book is thus both a group product and a very personal effort. Its dual origin is the reason the book has multiple authors on the cover but is written in the first person. The experiences, frameworks, and historical origins are mine. The main argument is very much the result of a shared effort. One nice feature of that dual origin is that although the book is primarily written by an old, white, North American male, the ideas were created and vetted by an extremely diverse set of individuals of more than twenty national origins, with a combination of race, age, religion, and personal identities too bountiful to enumerate. One thing I loved about collaborating with my colleagues on this book was the continuous challenge of attempting to find as balanced and multifaceted a perspective as possible, while maintaining a coherent storytelling voice. If a narrow perspective creeps in upon occasion, that is a failure on my part alone. My colleagues were wonderful in attempting to ensure that we had as many perspectives as possible weigh in on the ideas in this book. That is essential to our purpose, because we cannot claim that the whole world should be worried if many elements of the world were not part of creating these ideas.

Given the book is about the worries that concern all of us as citizens of our villages, towns, cities, countries, and the world, it could be said that the intended audience is everyone. But that perspective does not make for a very coherent book. Thus, while we hope any thoughtful reader will find value in what we have written, this volume is mostly intended for people who have a particular responsibility to address the worries and associated pending crises identified. The intended reader is either in a position to do something meaningful—that is, they are a leader of some key part of an organization, country, international association, state, province, city, institution, NGO (in other words, any organization that is a key part of our lives)—or they have particularly benefited by the lead-up to the crises and thus have the resources and experience to help navigate rethinking and repairing the things they helped break. For everyone else, the book offers a way of understanding the world we are all confronting, what we can help do about it, and—perhaps even more important—what we should demand of our leaders.

In some ways I have already revealed the core purpose of the book—to help us all understand the very real crises the world is facing and the urgency behind them and to suggest a set of ideas for what we can do about it. This brings me to the title of the book. As we came to understand the worrisome challenges, we encountered a striking pattern. For almost all of the issues, we have a decade to respond or things will get much worse. Even if we do not experience the absolute worst of the possible outcomes, if we do not identify how to address the crises and get a long way in dealing with them, we will face much more dire consequences. We really do have only *Ten Years to Midnight*.

Lastly, what can you expect in this book? All of the authors, save one, work for the world's largest professional services network, which includes the world's largest accounting practice. Thus you can expect evidence behind our assertions. We tried not to put in too many figures, but we could not make such bold assertions without evidence. These ideas emerged from hours of debate. Readers will find a host of arguments intended to bolster evidence and provide perspective. Each of the authors is a deeply caring human being. The most important parts of the book are the stories that reveal the consequences and the solutions, which will require individuals with courage and insight to make them happen. Expect a blend of story, argument, and evidence. Our hope is that we got the balance just right so those who like stories get enough of them, those who like data feel sated, and those who like a good framework or theory feel well treated.

In the end, even though this book is a joint effort, it is also very personal. The characters are people I have come to know personally and admire deeply, the places are all locales I care deeply about, and the messages are all ones I desperately hope we take to heart. I have two young granddaughters to whom I want to leave a healthy, wonderful world. If we do not address our crises, such a world won't exist, and that would be a terrible shame.

PART I

HOW WE GOT TO THE PRECIPICE

IN LIFE THERE ARE INFLECTION POINTS WHERE INACTION LEADS to the dramatic acceleration of something bad, but the appropriate action can produce a really good outcome. The world is at just such a point and we do not have much time to make the right choices and take the right steps.

The irony is that what has brought us to this inflection point are the forces that gave the world decades of amazing success. Since around 1950, in at least the Western, non-Soviet portion of the world (as well as in many countries with populations that aspired to be a part of it), we had generally agreed ideas emerging from the embers of the Second World War that guided us in confronting the challenges and taking advantage of the opportunities unique to the time. However, we became complacent and self-satisfied. As the years unwound, we lost the will to question the efficacy and outcomes of the choices we made after the war, and we failed to notice the ways in which technology and other forces were changing the systems we had built.

That was an enormous mistake. Today the consequences of our laserlike fealty to a graying world order are coming into disturbing focus: a set of extremely complex, far-reaching, and obstinate global problems that are already beyond simple responses. Indeed, because we have so far failed to credibly identify these problems—much less address them with urgency and new, imaginative answers—they have begun to mutate into dangerous crises. Crises that we must resolve now.

Throughout this book I describe these challenges in some depth and offer creative solutions. I came to identify these crises through an interesting route. Based on a general sense that the world had become a worrisome place, I visited with leaders in politics, business, and civil society as well as with individuals in coffee shops, hotels, schools, airports, buses, and taxis around the world. I asked them how they were feeling about the future. I learned that people were very worried and they all had consistent deep concerns. To summarize these repeated worries, my team and I coined the acronym ADAPT:

> **A**symmetry. Increasing wealth disparity and the erosion of the middle class.

> **D**isruption. The pervasive nature of technology and its impact on individuals, society, and our climate.

> **A**ge. Demographic pressure on business, social institutions, and economies.

> **P**olarization. Breakdown in global consensus and a fracturing world, with growing nationalism and populism.

> **T**rust. Declining confidence in the institutions that underpin society.

One worry I was surprised people didn't raise in our conversations was fear of a pandemic. When trying to find a path through the issues addressed in ADAPT, a pandemic would generate two new concerns: how to recover and prepare for the next one and how to deal with the very real political and economic consequences of the decisions taken to address it. It would be another massive disruption, and we would need to accommodate ourselves to its impact just as we will to the other forces described in this book. Indeed, a pandemic would cut across all the elements of ADAPT and risk accelerating them by, for example, hastening the increase of disparities within and between nations and causing a deeper questioning of the trust-worthiness of the institutions we have built to manage our lives.

But just singling out these shared worries without using data to deter-mine whether what people are worried about is actually cohering into a legitimate crisis was not sufficient. Thus, joined by the other authors, I set out to examine more concretely these recurring concerns. The result of that work is Part 1 of this book.

We learned that the ADAPT framework was on to something very real. The combination of wealth disparity, the perils of technology, countries aging at different rates, the breakdown in society, and the loss of trust is be-hind the emergence of four crises: a crisis of prosperity, a crisis of technol-ogy, a crisis of institutional legitimacy, and a crisis of leadership. Moreover, as each crisis worsens, it poisons other elements of ADAPT, multiplying the negative impact. ADAPT and its associated crises blend together into a pernicious system.

If we allow disparity to widen and sustain for too long, the risk is that a large number of people will simply give up, thinking that their lives will never improve. But prosperity requires the opposite: that people believe in the future and thus energetically create, work, invest, and build. When belief is lost, innovation to improve society diminishes and technology be-comes less of a force for good. This, combined with young countries hav-ing limited opportunities to offer their youthful, working-age populations, can lead to unrest, which spreads quickly around the world.

If we are not prepared to manage the negative consequences of ubiqui-tous technology or develop technology that elevates our cultures, our ca-pacity for cooperation, and our lives, society irreparably splinters into large and small cliques born of self-protecting individualism. To take advantage of these riven societies, political leaders on all sides promote unyielding partisanship rather than thoughtful, inclusive ideas that can improve the lives of many rather than a small base of constituents. In this environ-ment, institutions are neglected or even actively undermined, lose their

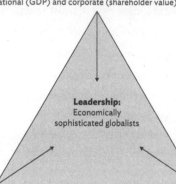

Strategy: Global interconnectivity with singular measures of success at the national (GDP) and corporate (shareholder value) levels

Leadership: Economically sophisticated globalists

Structure: Institutions built to sustain multilateralism, free markets, and technological interconnectivity

Culture: Market-based, technology focused

FIGURE P1.1 **The shared global alignment that drove seventy years of success following World War II.** SOURCE: Created by the authors.

relevance, and are used as political pawns, even though they are essential to the effective functioning of society. If we continue to fracture in this way and lose faith in the future, society, our leaders, and our institutions, essential changes that can eliminate the pall that hangs over us will never occur.

To explore more concretely how we have arrived at this inflection point (and what we should do about it), it is useful to view change through a simple model that I have drawn upon throughout my career as a teacher, leader, and adviser (Figure P1.1). To transform an organization, institution, even a society, four elements must be aligned: strategy, structure, culture, and leadership.

In the wake of World War II, the economies of countries around the globe were decimated and needed to be rebuilt from the ground up. Led in large part by the United States–backed Marshall Plan, which provided the money for European nations outside of the Soviet sphere to put their most severe economic woes behind them, a globally interconnected economy was spawned for the first time, based on this transformation model. The elements broke down this way:

> *Strategy.* Drive globalization and interconnected market economies using these metrics of success: Gross Domestic Product (GDP) for countries and shareholder value for companies.

> *Structure.* Build institutions to support growth of GDP and shareholder value as well as the principles of this change model, emphasizing free markets, multilateralism, and technological interconnectivity.

> *Culture.* Operate to maximize the success of markets as defined by very specific measures and continually strive for the next technological innovation to promote efficiency and effectiveness.

> *Leadership.* Develop people to become economically sophisticated globalists, placing emphasis on GDP and shareholder value as the key metrics determining a leader's success and expanding influence across the world.[1]

The years 1986–1992 represented a watershed period when this global network model became turbo-charged. In 1986 the City of London was deregulated, which in turn led to a massive liberalization of capital markets everywhere. Two years later, the World Wide Web was created, unleashing an open electronic communications and information forum that would facilitate in ways never before seen global interaction and innovation. In 1989 the Berlin Wall fell and a host of new countries that had been behind the Iron Curtain developed some form of market economy and entered the global community. Three years after that, Deng Xiao Ping's "southern tour" ensured that China would adopt market-based reforms and global trade as the foundations of its economy, unleashing unprecedented growth in the world's most populated country.

Until 2007, this model seemed to be working, at least on the surface (Figure P1.2). Global GDP grew at a remarkable rate, bringing billions of people out of poverty, creating significant wealth throughout the world,

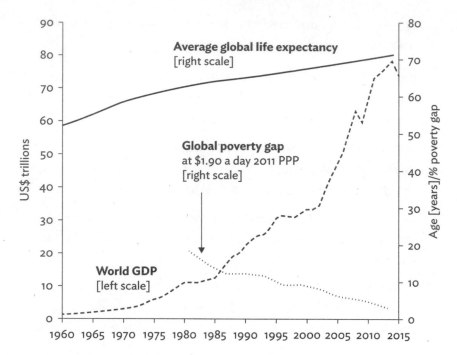

FIGURE P1.2 Economic and social progress since 1960.

SOURCE: databank.worldbank.org.

and increasing overall health and well-being. In the two decades since the late 1980s more than half the world's population had entered the global economy, buoying developing countries as well as the developed countries to which they sold their products and services.

But the financial crash in 2008 and the ensuing worldwide recession revealed the emerging dark underbelly of that success, which had been lost in the euphoria surrounding the postwar economic and social advances. The downturn brought out of the shadows the many people who were not receiving benefits from the global economic order anymore and the disconnect between them and the more privileged individuals and entities still profiting. The collapse in equities, housing, and capital markets swelled the ranks of the disadvantaged, making them even harder to ignore. This

post-2007 period is when the global problems and people's worries identified by the ADAPT framework began to make themselves known. To
further explain:

> **A**symmetry. One of the gains of globalization was that labor rates
  were normalizing around the world. This was great for people in
  emerging nations and for owners of capital in developed nations, but
  not for those who lost their jobs or who had stagnant wages due to
  globalization in places like France, the United Kingdom (UK), and
  the United States, where manufacturing used to be a desirable job
  with decent salaries and benefits. At the individual and regional levels,
  globalization was a core cause of asymmetry.

> **D**isruption. Rapidly accelerating technological innovation has caused
  disruption in many ways. The Internet helped create global platforms
  for economic exchanges and transfer of information, thus spawning
  new businesses and increasing efficiency dramatically. But it also
  disrupted traditional industries, which had often employed the people
  whose lives had already been harmed by globalization. In addition,
  advancements in technology that have made our lives easier have
  accelerated climate change and threatened our very existence.

> **A**ge. Such upheaval in the job requirements in major industrial
  and service sectors is just one of the ways that age (countries with
  populations that are increasingly too old or too young) exacerbates the
  challenges inherent in the ADAPT framework.

> **P**olarization. While simple measures such as shareholder value for or-
  ganizations and GDP for nations offered an easy way to keep score and
  make capital investment decisions, they also created a singular focus
  on economic success to the exclusion of social well-being, missing the
  very real problems being experienced by large swathes of people who
  became disenfranchised. This led to increasing polarization, which was
  amplified by the unintended consequences of technology.

▸ **Trust.** As disillusionment has grown and optimism about the future has ebbed, institutions (a wide-ranging term that includes tax systems, universities, the police and the military, and government agencies, to name just a few) have struggled and often failed to offer any solace or stability to people caught in the crossfire of these negative trends. That has precipitated a perilous loss of trust in institutions and leaders.

It is an intriguing accident that for each of these crises, we have ten years to respond: billions of African youths will reach working age by 2030; the protests ranging from the Gilets Jaunes to those in Hong Kong are harbingers of larger protests and global fracturing to come; continued inaction toward climate change for ten more years will likely produce irreversible consequences; large groups of retirees that will make big demands on government budgets will predominate in ten years; institutional failure will be at a breaking point in ten years; and technology platforms and their consequences will likely have rewritten the rules of manufacturing and most service industries by 2030. We have ten years to midnight. And the clock is ticking.

It is not that we have ten years to start the process of solving these crises. No, we have ten years to mostly address these crises. This will not be a simple task. It requires completely rethinking assumptions that for upwards of seventy years seemed self-evident. We have to reframe our ideas about political economies, reshape the institutions that once made our societies work, rein in technology and platforms that harm us while elevating the good, and find a way to bring a fractured world together. And do all of that at a scale that is rarely addressed over centuries, let alone ten years.

Part 2 of this book offers some solutions we could adopt to address the crises. They are not exhaustive—many more people and many more ideas will be needed to address all the challenges the world is facing—but they are a start. None of the solutions we propose works on its own; together, they form a system. Without addressing each crisis, we will fail to make progress on all of them as a cluster. Any individual or organization might, of course, focus on one or other of these potential solutions, because it is more relevant to the particular circumstances they find themselves in. As global citizens collectively we need to perceive of them as a group.

These chapters can therefore be thought of as a proposal to reframe the dominant logic still driving after all these decades our concepts of growth in the world, countries, regions, cities, and organizations. Certainly we should retain the basic elements of the past seventy years or so that still serve us well. But we should eliminate strategies that produce only negative outcomes now; we should update our thinking, our institutions, and our behaviors to attend to the very different realities that we face today.

As you read this book and give some thought to our collective worries and their associated crises, keep three things in mind. First, these are shared concerns that may vary in form around the world, but they are pervasive, affecting us and people in our communities everywhere. Thus solving them will require the participation of leaders and citizens from places big and small. It is not useful for people in one region to punt on a problem because they are not the primary cause of it.

Second, realigning global attitudes to a more shared and cooperative vision, as that vision is evolving today, will take time. Yet some of these issues are very big and strikingly urgent. They cannot wait for a new system of ideas and global relationships to emerge before being confronted. Hence, to borrow an oft-used analogy, we have to rebuild the plane while we are flying it. Even as we immediately address the most urgent issues, we must design solutions that accelerate the development of equally important long-term and ongoing needs, such as building and reinvigorating essential institutions, forging shared cultural and social bonds, rekindling innovation for social good, and reviving support for imaginative and open-minded leaders.

Which leads to my third point: solving today's global crises will involve steering through apparent paradoxes. We need to do things that may seem inherently at odds with each other. Let me offer two examples. In Part 2, I argue that we must place a much greater emphasis on local economies and politics than we do now. Yet we cannot ignore enormous global issues that are by definition too large and interwoven throughout every region in the world to be managed by local efforts; nor can we neglect the wider interdependencies that even local programs must navigate.

Similarly, if we hope to build technology that enhances the global community and serves as a bulwark against the challenges that can harm us, we need to develop in schools and organizations people who are technically capable but also studied in human nature and how systems facilitate and impact our lives. Generally we are not doing that now. How many engineering programs do you know that also teach sociology, political science, and psychology? How many humanities students also have expertise in computer science and engineering?

With these rules of the road in hand, let's see where this takes us. As you learn about our shared worries and the precipitating crises, it is my hope that ideas for action will surface so that the solutions will jumpstart, influence, motivate, and boost the steps that you are already thinking of taking.

CHAPTER 1

What Worries Us

The inspiration for this book was a single conversation that grew into hundreds of exchanges with people from all walks of life everywhere around the world. The conversation was in 2016 with Bob Moritz, chairman of the PwC International Network. Just a year and a half earlier, in my role as global leader for strategy and leadership at PwC, I led the development of the network's strategy—typical content such as what makes us distinctive, which capabilities do we need, and which markets should we focus on. This strategy was linked to a set of trends we believed would have a meaningful impact on the world in the coming years. These trends included such things as urbanization, shift in economic power from West to East, resource scarcity, and so on.

When Moritz and I spoke, we had just returned from separate trips to countries on four different continents. We both came back with the same nagging feeling—the world had gotten gritty and people seemed more on edge and anxious than we could ever recall in our lives. In other words, it was notably darker than the place we envisioned in 2015. Moritz asked a fundamental question: "What are people really worried about and does that affect how we should think about our business?" Answering that led me to spend the next two years in a whirlwind of conversations with leaders from government, business, and civil society as well as everyday people trying to make a decent living and build a better life for themselves and their children.

From coffee shops to boardrooms, I tried to find out how people felt about their lives and their perception of the future. Remarkably, I learned during these discussions that people in every country, at all levels of society, were in fact deeply worried. Much of what I heard is memorable, if a bit disturbing. To my surprise, there was more insecurity and pessimism than I had expected to find.

I was speaking with Amit Chandra, chairman of Bain Capital in India, about the development struggles in his country. In the middle of a lengthy discussion, Chandra said: "We do run the risk of having a revolution in India." I was struck by that comment. "Revolution" is a big word and Chandra is no radical; indeed, his private equity company could serve as the very icon for the global capitalist establishment and he is an extremely studied man. Chandra is also a prolific philanthropist, who aims to give away up to 90 percent of his wealth to nonprofits working to improve rural development as well as capacity building in the social sector, health, and education.[1] From that perch Chandra could see that something was unwinding at the core of the world's largest democracy.

The signs that India could suffer a revolution, Chandra told me, are obvious in the growing manifestations of extreme wealth and unrelenting poverty, sometimes right next to each other. Expensive private homes sit beside the largest slums in Mumbai. Some parts of India are rapidly leaving other parts behind. For instance, technology clusters in a variety of cities are training a new generation of technology leaders and buoying the efforts of digital entrepreneurs, increasingly consolidating wealth and inordinate national influence in these privileged areas. At the same time, conditions for subsistence farmers with little education and chances of social mobility are worsening; in some places, irrigation dams that small farmers depend upon are operating at 40 percent of capacity.

The week before the Brexit vote in the United Kingdom in May 2016, I heard a parallel story of people who feel powerless while their quality of life declines. In a taxi going from Manchester to Liverpool, the driver, who was from Liverpool, told me that he was very concerned about the outcome of the referendum. He considered his vote the most important of his life. He was choosing Leave because under the European Union, he said, his life was being altered for the worse by people he did not know, whom he could not influence, and who felt no accountability toward him. There was more: Two of the taxi driver's friends had given up their fishing businesses because of the catch limits imposed upon them. Violent crime near his home was increasing, the local pubs and restaurants he liked were closing, and good jobs in rural areas were getting harder to find. Liverpool, he said, had become unrecognizable, its ways of life no longer sustainable. He blamed all of this on decisions made in Brussels. "It's taxation and control without representation," he said. "You started a war over that in America, didn't you?"

I asked if he recognized the possible economic effect of an EU exit. The taxi driver mused: "Will it be worse than the consequences of the Second World War? We survived that." World war. Revolution. The strident language was striking. And omnipresent.

In a coffee shop in Madrid, across from the university, I overheard at the table next to me about a dozen students having a loud and energetic conversation about, of all things, what it would take to start World War III. I asked if I could join in and told them my interest was not so much in how to start the next all-in global conflict but rather in what has gotten them to the point that they want to fantasize about it.

That sparked an equally enthusiastic discussion that centered primarily on these points, as they put it: we have almost no chance of getting a job after graduating (the unemployment rate among Spanish youths is close to 50 percent); Euro currency arbitrage in the EU has essentially put Spain under the thumb of northern countries like Germany and France, unable to afford to make investments that would improve the economic and lifestyle prospects of its residents; Spain's technological base is falling behind other countries, making Spain less competitive globally; Spain is aging quickly and we, the young people, are going to have to support senior citizens in their retirement, but with what? Finally, the students told me, we simply do not trust our government or leaders of other institutions to do anything about it.

"So, what else should we do but figure out a way to wipe it all out and start over?" one student asked.

Not all of my hundreds of conversations were as pessimistic as the one I had with these Spanish students, but nearly everyone I spoke to was equally preoccupied with seemingly perilous and unyielding trends, and stumped about how to construct a palatable future. Among the noteworthy outcomes of the discussions with this diverse group of global correspondents, each extraordinarily unique, was that my question—What worries you the most?—elicited hundreds of different individual stories describing a wide array of circumstances and challenges (some daunting, some worse than that), but pared to their core the concerns raised were actually indistinguishable. They spoke in different tongues with wildly different inflections but ultimately portrayed problems that belied language barriers, identical in every corner of the globe.

Indeed, the things that worry us as individuals, it turns out, worry all of us as citizens of the world. Global problems are local problems and no different in North or South America, Europe, Asia, or Africa. After carefully going over the rich content in these conversations, I realized that what worries us today—and what we must focus our attention on to deliver a future that we would want to live in and that our children deserve to have—can be divided into the five ADAPT categories:

> **A**symmetry. Increasing wealth disparity and the erosion of the middle class.

> **D**isruption. The pervasive nature of technology and its impact on individuals, society, and our climate.

> **A**ge. Demographic pressure on business, social institutions, and economies.

> **P***olarization*. Breakdown in global consensus and a fracturing world, with growing nationalism and populism.

> **T***rust*. Declining confidence in the institutions that underpin society.

Although that tidy conclusion was compelling, as a former academic interacting with thousands of accountants on a day-to-day basis, I didn't feel that we could claim to construct an accurate profile of global concerns solely from an informal survey, no matter how consistent the results or how broad the sample. Thus my team and I set out to determine the validity of these worries. Should people really be concerned about ADAPT? Does the data actually support their unease? We worked with colleagues from a variety of PwC territories—including Australia, Brazil, Canada, China, Germany, Hungary, India, Italy, Japan, Mexico, the Middle East, Russia, Spain, South Africa, the UK, and the United States—to examine the degree to which the elements of ADAPT were present in their countries and in what form. Here is a brief review of the results of this exercise.[2]

Asymmetry

For the first time in recent history, a large percentage of parents believe that their children will be worse off than they are, chiefly because of the growing inequality in evidence today. As shown in Figure 1.1, fewer than 1 percent of the world's adults hold over 45 percent of the world's wealth and the number of billionaires is increasing—it more than doubled, from 1,125 to 2,754, between 2008 and 2018.[3] Moreover, in the industrialized countries of the Organization for Economic Cooperation and Development (OECD), the size of middle-income groups (those with a household net income between 0.75 and 2 times the median) has consistently decreased since 1988. The share of population that self-identifies as belonging to the middle class has fallen significantly—in the United States and Canada, for example, from two-thirds to one-half of the population since 2008.[4]

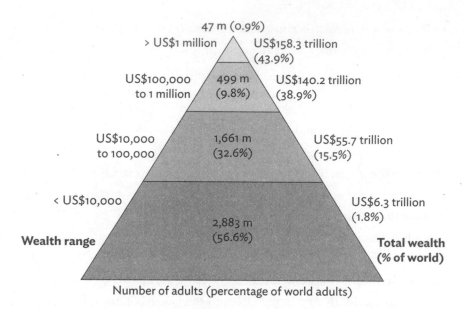

FIGURE 1.1 The global wealth pyramid, 2019. SOURCE: James Davies, Rodrigo Lluberas, and Anthony Shorrocks. Credit Suisse global wealth databook 2019.

A primary factor driving both the emergence from poverty and increasing income disparity is the shift of work from higher-wage to lower-wage countries—that is, the fundamental element of globalization. Given that billions of people have emerged from poverty as a result of this process, on the surface it would seem hard to criticize. Wealth has simply been distributed from countries that had more than enough to spare to those with the greatest need.

The problem is that not all parts of the countries that contributed wealth did so evenly and neither did all parts of the countries that received wealth. As an example, consider the distribution of gains in GDP in the developed countries, those that offshored labor. In developed economies, shareholder value grew nearly 18 percent from 1999 to 2015, while real wages grew only about 8 percent.[5] Said differently, those who owned companies gained much more than those who worked for them. As for the receiving

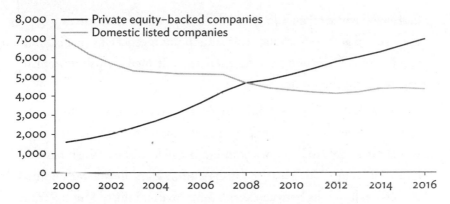

FIGURE 1.2 United States: Number of domestic listed versus private equity–backed companies, 2000–2016. SOURCE: World Bank, World Federations of Exchanges Database; Pitchbook.

countries, India provides a useful example. While the overall GDP of the country has increased from around $500 billion to $3 trillion between 1990 and today, the difference between median income in the three richest and three poorest states grew from 50 percent in 1990 to more than 300 percent today. These poorer states are really poor, with many people living at subsistence levels.

A valuable way to gauge economic asymmetry is through the primary vehicles of wealth creation: investments, home ownership, and wealth redistribution.

➤ *Investments.* As wealth disparity grew over the past few years, a growing number of wealthy investors have moved their money from public capital markets to private equity markets. These generally give better returns but are open to only accredited investors. To be accredited in the United States means you make at least $200,000 per year or have $1 million in net worth excluding property. To make matters worse, the number of publicly traded companies is shrinking throughout the developed world (Figure 1.2), and the percentage of individuals who are invested is also shrinking. This latter point is especially disturbing, as many people depend on investments in a defined contribution plan to provide for their retirement.

> *Home ownership.* The rise in house prices in much of the developed world suggests that many people currently under the age of forty will never be able to buy homes and thus will lose one of the main means of accumulating wealth for the middle class. In Australia home ownership by adults between ages twenty-five and thirty-four fell from 52.2 percent to 38.6 percent between 1995 and 2014, while the home ownership rate of people over sixty-five stayed constant.[6]

> *Wealth redistribution.* High wealth disparity also challenges a government's ability to collect tax revenues and therefore to provide services to those that need them the most. People with extreme wealth translate very little of it into income (income tax), consume far less proportional to their wealth than most of us do (consumption tax), and hold real estate in many locations and often in their corporations (real estate tax). Moreover, they are far more able to move their money across tax regimes to locate their wealth in low tax countries or states enabled by technology.

Disruption

Like economic asymmetry, technological disruption has a positive side. Without it, breakthroughs in medicine, material science, nanotechnology, and computing that have greatly improved the quality of life and lifespans, democratized the availability of valuable information, enhanced educational resources, and turned a big world into a small one would have been impossible. But the negative consequences of disruption—and the scale of the challenges from it—are so potentially palpable that unchecked they could easily outweigh the good.

The most obvious concern stemming from disruption involves the loss of jobs due to artificial intelligence, robotics, and virtual reality. However, less obvious but potentially more troubling is the impact technological advances since the Industrial Revolution are having on our climate, which I will discuss in more detail in later chapters.

The combination of these disruptive forces is unraveling many of the institutions that have traditionally been a bedrock of society and the reliable centerpiece of a community. These institutions—education systems, governments, public services, utilities, media, and so many more—have generally been in existence for a long time and in part gained the trust of people because they were designed to change slowly, to be solid, reliable entities that could provide sustained value to customers, individuals, families, neighborhoods, and nations. But technology is so roiling these institutions that their steadiness and constancy are increasingly perceived as shortcomings, signs that their usefulness is limited and their relevance is minimal.

The news media is a good example. Before the late 1990s, the basic business model for news was simple: audience members subscribed to a newspaper, magazine, or TV channel, and the media owner supplemented that revenue with advertising. This steady income enabled news providers to employ professional journalists who followed a clear set of rules about what constituted good reporting. Stability made news media credible. The time it took to write, publish, produce, and distribute an article or broadcast provided layers of filters that could detect inaccuracies or made-up news.

The Internet changed all that. Seeking the efficiency of targeted advertising with trackable responses and 24/7 access to consumers, marketing budgets moved to the platform companies such as Facebook, Twitter, and Tencent. After all, that is where the readers are. More than 50 percent of Americans get their news from social media or other online sources, many of which are of dubious quality.[7] Which means that news consumption shifted to material intended, first and foremost, to attract attention: negative stories and stories that told people what they wanted to hear, at the expense of accuracy.

The consequence. We have an increasingly polarized audience, widespread skepticism about the integrity of the media, and no generally accepted way to tell "fake news" from real. Indeed, Facebook has gone so far as to say that on its platform—one of the world's most influential information-dissemination environments *ever*—the difference between presenting lies and truths doesn't exist anymore. And, in fact, shouldn't. Despite criticism, the company has vociferously defended a policy that allows obviously false political ads to run unconstrained next to ones that strive for accuracy.[8]

Trust or (Better Put) the Extreme Lack of It

Institutional distrust is a worldwide phenomenon. In nearly every region of the globe people have lost faith in the credibility of governments, corporations, media, universities, and religious organizations. A significant amount of the loss of trust reflects bad behavior: the financial crisis, institutional leaks, political corruption, police bias and brutality, and a wide range of public disclosures of egregious acts by corporate leaders and icons have all contributed.

The Edelman Trust Barometer, which has tracked the perception of institutional credibility since 2001, presents a sobering picture. In 2020 twelve of the twenty-six countries surveyed had trust scores below 50 percent—meaning that the majority of people responding in each of these countries distrusted its major institutions. In the United States alone, the 2018 result represented "an 18-year low in trust across government, business, media and NGOs...the steepest, most dramatic decline we've ever seen," according Rob Regh, chairman of US public affairs at Edelman. Although the US trust score rose in 2019, it skidded again in 2020. But even with the improvements in 2020, the survey found a record 14-point gap in trust scores (65 percent versus 51 percent) between the informed public and the mass population, with eight countries posting record levels of trust inequality (Figure 1.3).

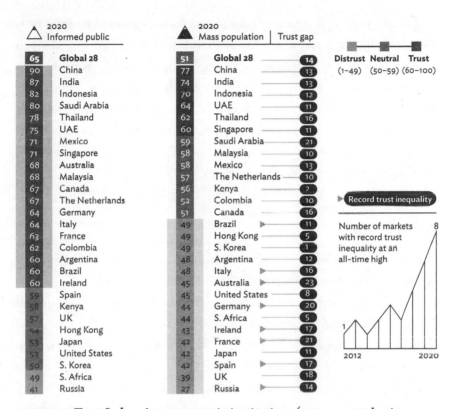

FIGURE 1.3 Trust Index: Average trust in institutions (government, business, NGOs, and media). SOURCE: 2020 Edelman Trust Barometer, page 6.

Among the big exceptions were China and India, where more than two-thirds of those surveyed felt that institutions in all categories were worthy of their trust, and where improving economic conditions have convinced their citizens that institutions are working for them. More than likely those numbers have slipped in China and India in the past two years as their economic growth has slowed, social safety nets and the ability of the national governments to maintain basic quality-of-life standards in local communities have been tested, and political turmoil has surfaced, particularly in Hong Kong and Kashmir.

The net result of institutional distrust globally is a broad body of people who maintain a skeptical view of their future and of anyone charged with shepherding it. Consider, for example, the Gilets Jaunes protests in France in 2019 in which no solution was considered sufficient. The deeper issue at the heart of the protests was the lack of faith in the institution of government itself. Without some trustworthy institutions—organizations that not only earn and deserve trust but continue to improve in order to not lose it—civil society cannot function.

Polarization

The three primary worries already described—economic disparity, technological disruption, and institutional distrust—combine to produce a fourth bucket: namely, polarization including the allure of false or real populists and the resulting division within society and across nations. Consider how people respond to their heightened concerns. First, they say: "I want the world to look like it did. I was more optimistic in the world I knew before." Second, they close in, rallying around people like themselves who are also experiencing the world the same way. Third, they blame those in power—the elites—for stoking their unease and fueling their uncertainties. These are not the behaviors of irrational people, but the understandable reaction of people who feel the future is likely to be worse than the past. It is the perfect seed culture for populism and nationalism (the frequent by-product of faux populism).[9]

As nationalism expands its reach into every continent, its perils become more obvious. For instance, populist political leaders often take aim at migrants, blaming them for stealing local jobs, crime waves, and overusing social services. It doesn't matter that these claims have been disputed by nearly every major study, which instead hold that immigration is almost always a boon to local economies, adding to the pool of younger workers, and powering increases in consumer activity. But by tarring the immigrant population as being harmful and destructive, nationalist leaders hope to achieve their true aims: driving tribalism in their midst and fracturing consensus or at least minimizing dialogue among their communities so that they can control the beliefs and biases of their constituencies.

Age

Age and population growth are the unseen eight-hundred-pound gorillas in the room, the invisible but potent forces that can accelerate the dynamics and negative consequences of economic disparity, technological disruption, institutional distrust, and polarization. Simply put, demographics is a global time bomb with an uncertain capacity.

The world population, which was just more than three billion in 1960, has ballooned to about eight billion people who are divided in two very different groups. One group comprises countries with large populations of young people. Places like India, where nearly 65 percent of the population is younger than thirty-five. The country has an opportunity to drive economic growth on the back of its rising working-age population, which has grown by 2 percent compounded annually since 2000 (often referred to as India's demographic dividend) and should surpass one billion by 2030. However, whether India can actually generate the millions of jobs needed to put these young people to work is an open question that has attracted plenty of skeptics. If India fails at that, unemployment and dissatisfaction will be rampant among a very large segment of the country.

The rest of the world includes nations whose populations are shrinking and aging rapidly (most of Europe and, notably, Japan). In these countries the tax base of working-age people will have to expand greatly to cover the intensifying demands for retirement support and healthcare of a swelling over-sixty-five population.

What makes demographic trends a particularly dicey factor is the role they can play in exacerbating the least desirable impacts of the direst global trends. For instance, because of demographics, the divide between rich and poor could worsen in countries unable to provide social services for their old (if the nation is aging) or jobs for their young (if that is the dominant segment). That would fracture societies even more, pitting older, more conservative adults against restive youth unable to find a silver lining in any future scenario. Technological disruption might provide jobs for young, digitally oriented workers but at the expense of older folks replaced by machines. Nativism among older populations in developed countries could also become more prevalent in response to large numbers of young migrants seeking opportunities in countries that traditionally create jobs. Ultimately the failure of institutions to address the pressing needs of young and old would further aggravate distrust of institutions around the world.

◎ ◎ ◎

This brief survey of ADAPT, combined with the data that supports it, establishes pretty clearly that people's concerns are well-founded. As we plumb these issues further, something else even more disconcerting comes into focus: namely, what people say they are worried about actually foreshadows a pending set of crises, each of which, if not addressed within the next decade, is likely to result in outcomes of far greater consequence.

Asymmetry	...the Crisis of Prosperity
Disruption	...the Crisis of Technology
Trust	...the Crisis of Institutional Legitimacy
Polarization	...the Crisis of Leadership
Age	...Accelerating the Four Crises

Each crisis is urgent and must be responded to immediately with creativity, imagination, and stubborn persistence. We have only ten years to turn the tide away from these crises—or we may lose the opportunity. The following chapters delve deeply into the crises, charting their characteristics and the nature of their threat. The second part of the book offers solutions. I am not an alarmist, but I am deeply worried.

CHAPTER 2

Asymmetry and the Crisis of Prosperity

If the crumbling of the Berlin Wall and the fall of the Soviet Union was supposed to signal "the end of history," as political scientist Francis Fukuyama famously declared, and the dawning of a period dominated by global liberal democracies and marked by economic opportunities for everyone, you could have fooled the people of the city of Hamilton, Ontario, where I was born and raised.[1]

Throughout much of the 1900s, Hamilton was one of those Rust Belt boomtowns, primarily owing its prosperity to two global steelmaking companies, Stelco and Dofasco. Wages were good for industrial workers, who could afford small houses nearby and reasonably expect their children to attend college and live better lives than theirs. The middle class expanded enormously—the population grew from 253,000 in 1950 to 591,000 in 1990.[2] The community was vibrant, the site of the Canadian Football Hall of Fame, theaters, museums, and the highly regarded McMaster University with its renowned medical school.

But as the Soviet Union slipped into the past, this version of Hamilton did also. Canada's steel industry collapsed as globalization shifted the locus of the sector to lower-wage countries and more efficient startup mini-mills. Hamilton steel workers had trouble finding new jobs and the work they found often paid poorly. Their neighborhoods became less desirable; their children's prospects bleaker. However, the well-worn tale of the industrial town ghosted by globalization is not Hamilton's story and is not what makes Hamilton illuminating for us today. Unlike, say, Detroit or Youngstown, Ohio, Hamilton actually does not look the worse for wear. On the whole, the streets are still clean, downtown is thriving, suburban communities are still growing up around the city, and the town appears to be flush and bustling. The reason is, as industry left, high-tech moved in.[3] And the region that founded its first winery in 1975 today has more than 102 wineries.[4]

I bring up Hamilton's rise, fall, and rebirth (which has echoes in other places like Pittsburgh in the United States and Birmingham in the United Kingdom) because it illustrates well the nuanced complexity of the crisis of prosperity. Despite the temptation to minimize its full impact by pigeon-holing it into familiar explanations, this crisis exists everywhere: it's a Rust Belt problem, a rural problem, a "third tier" city problem. These municipalities failed to keep up with global change.

Leaders in Hamilton did the right thing by engineering a transformation of the city away from the old world into the new. Yet that only whitewashed a bad situation and worsened economic disparity while masking it. Because of the tech bonanza in Hamilton, between 1982 and 2013 the paychecks of the top 1 percent of earners—those who earn more than CA$400,000 annually—have nearly doubled, according to Canada's Social Planning and Research Council. In contrast, the bottom 90 percent of earners, whose average wage is around CA$31,200 per year, are making only 2 percent more than they did in 1982 when adjusted for inflation. If anything, these trends have accelerated since 2013, as technology companies have become even more of a fixture in Hamilton.

This severe income gap in a town that you would not expect to be affected is a warning flag: the crisis of prosperity is pervasive, even when it is hard to see. Because it can sometimes be invisible, much more than simplistic analysis will be needed to understand the myriad characteristics of the crisis. Something besides one-size-fits-all answers will be necessary to wrestle it to the ground. But, we have no choice but to come to grips with this crisis. The threat to the world is significant. Unchecked, this crisis will infect (indeed, it already is infecting) our social, economic, and political systems in both large and less obvious ways.

When the general population is not prospering, societies are in deep trouble. Real and felt prosperity are absolute requisites for countries or regions to function effectively. When people do not feel prosperous, they don't buy, dream, launch new businesses, pay sufficient taxes, or otherwise contribute to growth. And they are more anxious, which results in greater amounts of drug and alcohol abuse, domestic violence, and self-harm, and less inclination to participate in routine community activities. Rather, when people do not feel prosperous, they become more insular, seeking out others like themselves. In turn, society fractures. Not surprisingly, people who have no hope for a better future draw the conclusion that those who are running the world (or those who just seem to be better off) are the cause of their misery—and the fissures among different economic and social strata widen. In desperation, people are more inclined to lash out by trampling on traditional norms and rejecting institutions that society needs to flourish.

Perhaps the best way to lay bare the layers of asymmetry in the world and explore their component parts—to develop targeted antidotes—is through the lens of the four leading geopolitical players that have dominated the world since the end of the Cold War: China, the European Union, Russia, and the United States. Each player vies for global spheres of influence using a variety of weapons—ranging from trade to regulation to currency to social media to military might—to outpace the other.

As this competition heats up, neglected or unaddressed by the global powers are their own notable crises of prosperity. Even as they strive to write the rules of engagement for the rest of the world, these nations and regions have three distinct segments of their populations with consequential challenges of prosperity that are only getting worse. Together these three cohorts form the vast majority of the population of each country or region. It is not to exclude the rest of the world that we focus on China, the European Union, Russia, and the United States, but if they are facing severe asymmetry, imagine what everyone else is going through.

Young and Falling Behind

As a former professor and dean, I have seen many people go off to start their careers all over the world. Some decades back, that rite of passage was a joyous one with a lot of optimism that these Duke graduates had nothing but blue skies ahead. If they made the right decisions, they would almost certainly succeed professionally and financially—and relatively quickly. I don't feel that way anymore. Recent college graduates trying to make their way in Berlin, Moscow, New York, or Shanghai confront remarkably similar challenges. These young people are living a life quite different from that of their parents a few decades earlier. In most cases, they are financially not for the better. There are several reasons for this.

First, young people today are having trouble keeping up with prior generations because of the high cost of shelter in major cities. Take, for instance, the larger cities in China (Figure 2.1). In Shanghai the cost of a house is just under forty times the annual income of an average worker. To put this in perspective, lenders typically advise against buying a house valued at more than three times a person's income. In London, New York, or Paris, average house price to income ratios are lower than in China but still well above desirable levels. Given these prices, it is not surprising that many young people view home ownership as an unreachable goal.

Some young professionals earning a good salary can find other ways to live decently in big cities through apartment sharing or other creative means. But many graduates cannot find well-paying jobs (working instead in lower-paying service industries as bartenders and as servers in restaurants, for example) and do not have this option. They have to accept substandard living conditions or long commutes that consume much of their discretionary income.

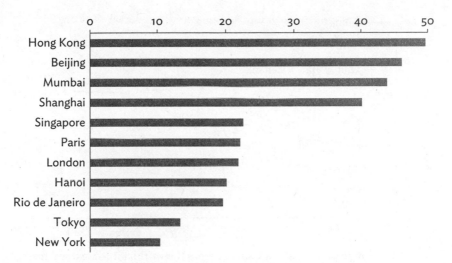

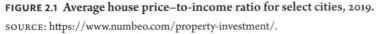

FIGURE 2.1 **Average house price–to-income ratio for select cities, 2019.**
SOURCE: https://www.numbeo.com/property-investment/.

Of course, not every region has the burden of high housing costs. For example, in Germany, fewer people are concentrated in major cities that attract the majority of young professionals; instead employment tends to be spread among midsized urban areas throughout the country. Consequently, real estate costs are relatively equal in cities with similar population sizes. That may be changing, though. Berlin is beginning to look a bit more like Paris and London every year; currently, the price-to-income ratio in Berlin has crept up to just over 10.[5] According to the *Moscow Times*, Moscow's real estate prices rose 8.9 percent in 2018, sixth in the world on CBRE's Global Living report, although the overall cost of living remains exceptionally low.[6]

The second reason young people are entering adulthood behind the eight ball concerns worsening disparities in who controls most of the wealth in a given region. It is the rare college graduate who enters the job market with a salary anywhere approaching the top income levels or with

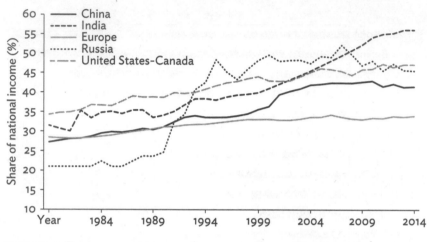

FIGURE 2.2 Top 10 percent income share across the world, 1980–2015. SOURCE:
https://wid.world/world/#sptinc_p90p100_z/US;FR;DE;CN;ZA;GB;WO/last/eu/k/p
/yearly/s/false/25.253500000000003/80/curve/false/country.

prospects of getting there soon. Those that do are outliers—perhaps they
invented something really important in high school or college, or they entered a thriving family business. The problem is, those on the top rung are
keeping more to themselves and this is not only a uniquely Anglo-American
or even a capitalist problem. Whether it be China, Europe, Russia, or the
United States, the line reflecting the percentage of the wealth held by the
top 10 percent has steadily grown since 1980 (Figure 2.2).

Adding to this cost-of-living challenge are rising debt levels for college
graduates. Graduates leave school not only confronting expensive housing but saddled with debt. The United States leads in this area with college
debt approaching $1.5 trillion. Things are a bit better in China, because
typically parents have sacrificed to help their child through college. Thus
college kids in China have a different kind of burden: the obligation to
be a success to pay back their parents' expensive belief in them. According to the *Financial Times*, UK university graduates have an average debt
of £44,000 (US $57,519) upon graduation, compared with £16,200 (US

$21,177) five years earlier.[7] Even in countries with no matriculation costs, students are still borrowing. In tuition-free Sweden, for example, 70 percent of graduates have student loans, typically totaling 172,000 kronor (US$18,174).[8]

The high cost of education would be palatable if students were being well-prepared for the future and there was good work available when they graduated. As someone who has worked on curriculum redesign throughout my career, I know two things to be true: (1) curricula are not just based on the needs of students but also the interests and political preferences of the faculty; and (2) curriculum redesign is a hard and slow process. In truth, the world is changing at a pace faster than curricula can keep up.

Finally, today's graduates are beginning their journey as tax-paying citizens in countries that are very old and getting older every year. At first glance, this could be seen as a good thing as their options for work are greater, there is less competition, and work is opening up due to an aging population, but consider the financial burden being handed to these graduates. As the population ages, the fraction of a person a single taxpayer will have to support through their taxes (the dependency ratio) will rise in concert. In the four regions we focus on here, this ratio began climbing around 2010 and will continue to grow through the century. The population group on the receiving end of this expensive demographic divide is the subject of the next section.

Retiring Broke

It is interesting to approach that point in life when one begins to ask the question, What would it be like to consume my savings rather than continue to contribute to them? I count myself as fortunate in this regard, because I have done pretty well in life and saved with this date in mind. Nonetheless, it is scary to contemplate potential black swan events that could wipe out a lifetime of savings or make them irrelevant, such as rampant inflation, deep depression, or global war. Yet there are many living

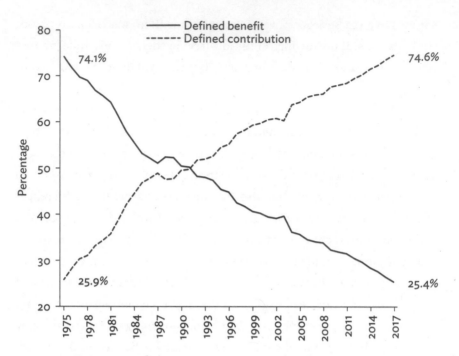

FIGURE 2.3 **Percentage of participants in pension plans by pension type,**
1975–2017. SOURCE: Department of Labor, Private Pension Plan Bulletin Historical Tables
and Graphs, 1975–2017.

in the four regions under discussion in this chapter who have much more
worrisome and immediate problems.

Let's start with the United States. In 1978, Congress created 401(k)
plans, which allow employees to avoid tax on deferred compensation
saved for retirement. On the face of it, these retirement accounts seem like
a plus, giving individuals an inexpensive way to set up personal pensions
by investing a part of their pretax earnings usually in mutual funds. Instead,
this well-intentioned program has taken an axe to the prosperity of many
retirees. Since 401(k)s were debuted, the percentage of US employees in
the United States with defined benefit plans—traditional pensions, where
people receive a guaranteed amount of money in retirement—fell from
just over 60 percent to approximately 10 percent from 1980 to 2006, while

the percentage with a 401(k)-like defined contribution plan grew from 17 percent to more than 65 percent, a complete reversal (Figure 2.3). In 2016, 54 percent of all of those employed in the United States had no plan whatsoever and only 8 percent were on a defined benefit pension plan. For the age group facing pending retirement—those between fifty and fifty-nine—46 percent had no plan and 9 percent had a defined benefit pension plan.[9]

In other words, more often than not, employers used the emergence of 401(k)s as a way to get out of the business of providing retirement pensions to workers (although some offer to match a portion of employee contributions) and an alarming number of workers have no plan and are entirely self-funding their retirement.

The problem with this shift—at least viewing it through the perspective of retiree economic well-being—is that investment decisions and even the decision to participate at all in saving for retirement have been transferred to employees, many of whom are deciding to do things like sustain their existing lifestyle or fund their children's increasingly expensive education by either drawing from their 401(k)s or not investing at all. In addition, the financial crash in 2008 decimated the value of 401(k)s, scaring a lot of individuals out of the market when their losses were at their worst. And many haven't returned. Indeed, the largest age group leaving the market was fifty-five to sixty-five, the cohort about to enter retirement.

What all of this means is that a large number of Americans will be retiring with no real reserves and thus depending primarily on Social Security, a system itself under real strain. According to a 2019 survey, 55 percent of respondents fifty-five to sixty-five had less than $10,000 saved for retirement and about 69 percent said they had less than $50,000.[10] This group will require additional support and resources not anticipated in the current system.

But what about Russia, the European Union, and China? I recently had the opportunity to take a river cruise from Moscow to Saint Petersburg with my wife and her siblings. Outside of the major cities, you find older

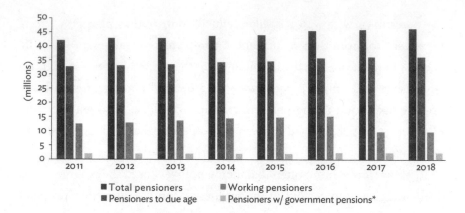

FIGURE 2.4 **Number of pensioners in Russia.** SOURCE: RBC Magazine, "Russia retired: how the situation of different types of pensioners in the country varies," Ivan Tkachv, Julia Statostina, Damir Yanayev. July 5, 2018. From data from Russian Federal State Statistic Service. wwww.rbc.ru/economics/05/07/2018/5b3b6t739a79175033464791.

people living under extremely difficult circumstances. The issue is not that they lack pensions. Rather, it is that the pensions are not adequate. Given Russian demographics, the country is not in a position to alleviate the problem. The number of pensioners has increased more than 10 percent since 2010, while the population growth was very small (1.4 percent) and is predicted to go into negatives, which puts significant pressure on the system to pay for the retirees.[11] During this period the Russian government has held the pension steady at an average of 13,100 rubles (US$175) per month, which is extremely difficult to live on. Consequently, many retirees continue to work (Figure 2.4).

Moving several hundred miles to the west, Scandinavia is considered by many to be a model of social progress and success, consistently winning accolades as the region with the most satisfied populations. Yet, even here, economic asymmetry affects the old. In the countryside, Finland, Sweden, and Norway are dotted with beautiful villages often on deep, clear lakes or

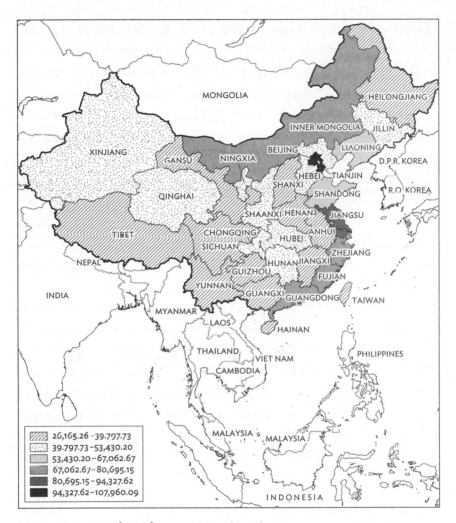

MAP 2.1 Per capita (RMB) gross regional product, 2015. SOURCE: National Bureau of Statistics of China; accessed on line January 13, 2020. http://data.stats.gov.cn/english/mapdata.htm?cn=E0103&zb=A0301. Redrawn by Bill Nelson.

fjords just a few hours from the major cities. Looking closely, you can see the origins of the Norse culture, a rugged existence in which people learn that they need to care for one another if they are to survive the harsh winter conditions.

But in most of these villages today the youth have left. They have gone to the cities, where jobs are available and life is more interesting. And, by and large, they did not take their parents with them. Instead, the youth took the grocery stores, banks, theaters, restaurants, doctors, and lawyers. Retirees left behind in these villages have to travel a long way to do such simple tasks as depositing money into a bank account, buying food, getting a haircut, or seeing a movie. Moreover, reasonably well-to-do retirees are getting tired of this diminished lifestyle and are leaving as well. Which means that only the least wealthy seniors have no choice but to stay and watch their homes drop in value as the village becomes less attractive. The world left them behind and seems not to care. This troubling scenario is not just taking place in the Nordic region; it is being replicated in most of western Europe as well as on the other side of the globe in Japan and China.

Regional economic disparity is a particularly difficult problem for those who cannot leave to try to overcome it. More often than not, that is the elderly. In China, for example, these misfortunate regions represent the country's largest land mass and a sizable population (Map 2.1). A map contrasting northern and southern Europe, Moscow and Saint Petersburg with the rest of Russia, and the coastal United States versus the interior would show similar disparities and clearly reveal regions where retired people feel trapped to live.

The Encumbered Middle

But surely life is good for those who sit between those two groups, those who are midcareer, who have time to save for retirement, are well beyond student debt if they ever had it, are fully into their careers, and have already found proper housing and a good job—right? They can't be worried about their own crises of prosperity. Hold that thought for a moment.

On my team I have people who would all be considered in the economically advantaged category. They live in Europe, Russia, and the United

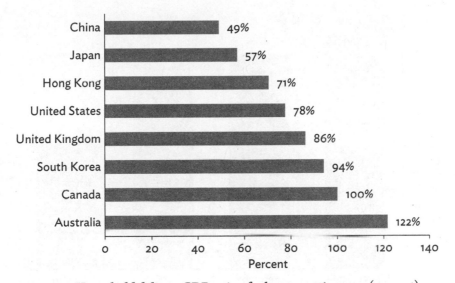

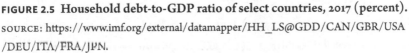

FIGURE 2.5 Household debt-to-GDP ratio of select countries, 2017 (percent).
SOURCE: https://www.imf.org/external/datamapper/HH_LS@GDD/CAN/GBR/USA
/DEU/ITA/FRA/JPN.

States. When we researched the idea of economic insecurity and its impact on people with partners in countries around the world, we clearly and relatively quickly identified the "young and falling behind" and the "retiring broke" as at risk. We debated how these issues relate to my team and their friends. We discovered that they—this third group that I have dubbed "the encumbered middle"—may be most exposed, even if it is not yet visible.

There's a lot going on in their economic lives. They have a mortgage and frequently a car payment (Figure 2.5). They have children in school, often at some great expense as they try to make life as good as possible for their kids. And they have parents who are increasingly dependent on them. In other words, this group is carrying not only their own expenses and liabilities, but as the economic problems of the other two groups described have worsened, the encumbered middle has had to fill in the financial gaps. It was a real surprise to me to hear the undertones of fear in the conversation

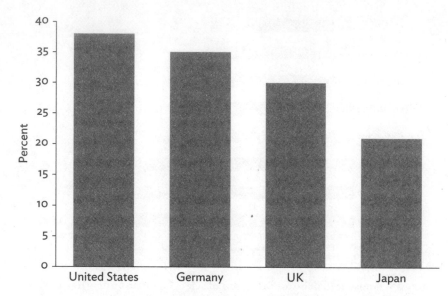

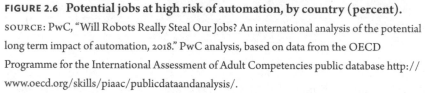

FIGURE 2.6 Potential jobs at high risk of automation, by country (percent).
SOURCE: PwC, "Will Robots Really Steal Our Jobs? An international analysis of the potential long term impact of automation, 2018." PwC analysis, based on data from the OECD Programme for the International Assessment of Adult Competencies public database http://www.oecd.org/skills/piaac/publicdataandanalysis/.

because I was surrounded by bright, sophisticated, and effective people; yet they've seen the data firsthand and know very well that for the want of a small change, "there too go I." For this group, even success in the present is shadowed by a nagging fear sitting just over their shoulder.

The encumbered middle has the highest need for cash flow, but it is also the group most exposed to the potential loss of work to artificial intelligence, robotics, and industry disruption. This is not just a Western problem; in fact, it may be most acute in China, where the cost of housing and education is already pushing most middle-class families to the limits of their budget. If they were laid off, which is a reasonably high risk everywhere around the world (Figure 2.6), even for a small period of time, they have little savings to fall back on. According to the *Financial Times*, the Chinese government's well-publicized push to automate and become a "world superpower" in AI has resulted in the elimination of up to 40 percent of the jobs in some industrial companies since 2015.[12]

I do not mean to imply that other kinds of work won't become available when these jobs go. However, the transition into new jobs for the encumbered middle will, if nothing else, be extremely challenging. No matter what their situation now, this group has a right to be worried about the future.

Prosperity Crisis in One Chart

This chapter paints a pretty worrisome picture for each of the four regions covered. Each is experiencing significant internal challenges that will grow more acute by 2030 and in many cases the challenges are not yet recognized. However, they are mutually reinforcing. Too many retirees lacking economic resources places a greater burden on the tax system, which puts additional strain on the encumbered middle. Too few people in the middle with the wherewithal to be active consumers leads to fewer good positions for young job seekers or too little tax revenue to support the region's growing need to expand services.

Table 2.1 summarizes the challenges the three population segments discussed in this chapter will likely confront over the next decade. And they are big. Big enough that there will probably be considerable political turmoil involving domestic policies and geopolitical stances growing out of the attempts to navigate a troubling future. Although the table shows some differences across countries and regions, it is striking how often these groups face the same worries wherever they are.

The central takeaway is that each of these groups is (and is feeling) less prosperous. That is a crisis in itself. No matter how serene, rosy, and even promising the surface of the picture looks—think Hamilton,

TABLE 2.1 Severity of challenges for three population segments, by region.

	United States	China	European Union	Russia
Young and falling behind				
Indebtedness	High	Low	Medium	Low
Unaffordable housing	Mixed	High	Low	Low
Tax burden	High	Medium	High	High
Quality of preparation for work	Mixed	Mixed	Mixed	Mixed
Retiring broke				
Underfunded retirement	High	High	Mixed	High
Regional disparity	Medium	High	High	High
Healthcare quality and cost	High	High	Low	High
Dependency ratio challenges	Medium	Medium	High	Medium
Encumbered middle				
Job transition risk	High	High	Medium	Medium
Challenge in sustaining lifestyle	Mixed	High	Mixed	High
Parental care/tax burden	High	High	High	High

Source: Created by the authors.

Ontario—when a large part of the population is deadly worried about how they will be able to afford to live in the present or the future, countries and regions rapidly deteriorate into dysfunction and ultimately lose sight of a path to prosperity.

CHAPTER 3

Disruption and the Crisis of Technology

The end of World War II marked the beginning of the period that re-sulted in remarkable economic and social progress but would eventually lead to the forces that drove the worries expressed around the world in the form of ADAPT (asymmetry, disruption, age, polarization, and trust). It also marked another important point in human history: with the advent of the nuclear bomb, we had created a technology that could eradicate us and much of the natural world. The planet and human society have seen massive disruptions before, but most of those have been the result of natural disasters or outbreaks of disease. When they were the consequence of war, the result was usually limited to a single major region or political system.[1] The potential disruptive consequences of a nuclear war required us to rethink how nations interact, how we protect ourselves from ourselves, and how we envision our relationship to each other.

Today we face a similar dilemma. The sheer ubiquity of rapidly and dynamically advancing technology in our lives and our societies threatens us and our environments in ways that are perplexing and seemingly intractable. Although technology certainly contributes to innumerable improvements in critical facets of our day-to-day existence, there are nonetheless two extremely dangerous risks that arise from the outsized role technology plays in our lives. The first is the disruptive impact of information technology on our daily existence and goals and aspirations. Chapter 5 focuses on the other, arguably greater, disruption: the basic technologies by which we generate energy, grow the food we eat, make and transport goods, go from one place to another, build the things we work and live in, and keep ourselves comfortable are making the world too hot.

IT Disruption and Harmful Effects on People and Society

If you ask a child to draw a robot, more than likely the picture will be of a boxy human—square face, eyes, ears, nose, mouth, and all of the same limbs as people. Meanwhile, since 1950, adults have been administering the Turing Test to computers of every ilk, trying to identify machines that have crossed over into the human sphere by whether they exhibit intelligent behavior indistinguishable from that of a person.

Both statements point to the distinctive relationship that people have with computers and the digital world. No other products or services are so identified with human intelligence, sharing our unique capacity for juggling complex groups of knowledge and information and—to a degree— our sentient characteristics. And none, not even the automobile, has the potential to so disrupt fundamental aspects of how we live and what matters most to us. As a result, over the years the role that new technology plays in our lives is constantly being adjusted and recalibrated, in an effort to balance the good it brings to society with its impact on critical human values involving privacy, livelihoods, quality of life, education, and the way people relate to our friends, families, and communities.

For decades, before the widespread use of the Internet and, importantly, before the more recent emergence of the huge technology platforms that dominate our economies—the Big Four in much of the world (Google, Amazon, Facebook, and Apple) and Baidu, Alibaba, and Tencent (BAT) in the rest—maintaining this balance was difficult but not impossible. Indeed, many of the efforts to bring new digital breakthroughs into our workplaces, homes, and social spaces were founded on the assumption that technology is benign, valuable, and certainly manageable.

But that conclusion is no longer so clear-cut (even among technologists themselves).[2] Precisely because digital technologies increasingly mirror characteristics of human intelligence, are more efficient than us, and are advancing at a speed that makes the past seem slothful, it is becoming harder to temper the disruptions in our lives engendered by new hardware, software, apps, and platforms. As a result, in nearly all industries as well as social, political, and economic circles, technology is freely rewriting assumptions that used to guide day-to-day activities, taking over essential tasks from people while offering new channels of communication and information of varying quality.

The sheer depth (and likelihood of a continuing wave) of technology-based disruptions is provoking a growing chorus of global worries about the threats posed by technology, a sentiment I heard from almost everybody I spoke to. The dangers of the sudden rise and global ubiquity of the giant technology platforms was uppermost in people's minds.[3] These companies have deftly built their business models on key attributes of technological success—from massive economies of scale, to an ability to accumulate vast amounts of data and use artificial intelligence to glean the most valuable information from that data, to completely reshaping the nature of shopping, media, healthcare, social relationships, and finance into a platform economy. As a result, substantial wealth, influence, consumer and personal data, and market control accrue to this small group of companies and those who run them. Meanwhile, other technological advances—for instance, in robotics artificial intelligence and virtual reality—are imperiling jobs and livelihoods.

To be sure, technology can be an extraordinarily positive force. Because of it, we get nearly everything better, cheaper, and faster. Goods and services can be tailored to our personal needs. We can do things we never imagined before. Tremendous amounts of knowledge are at our fingertips. New entrepreneurial industries are rising up to replace old and inefficient ones. The challenge is that because of technology's pervasiveness in our lives the harm that it can potentially do is also colossal in scale.

Simply put, we face a number of conundrums: how can we have the benefits of this new world and manage or mitigate the liabilities? To what degree should we hold technology companies accountable for negative outcomes stemming from their products? What is the responsibility of technology companies to police themselves from doing harm? How can we safeguard against technology changing us in detrimental ways? Or, as Apple CEO Tim Cook put it in a commencement address at MIT in 2017: "Technology is capable of doing great things, but it doesn't want to do great things. That part takes all of us.... I'm not worried about artificial intelligence giving computers the ability to think like humans. I'm more worried about people thinking like computers without values or compassion, without concern for consequences." This chapter elaborates on the most salient threats that new technology and digitization pose. Later chapters discuss how to tackle these threats.

Wealth Disparity

Duke University professor Phil Cook and his coauthor, Robert Frank, were among the first to identify a core characteristic of the economy: it has increasingly become "winner take all."[4] Their argument was that in a highly networked, knowledge-rich, platform-based world, a few at the top are disproportionately compensated because their place atop the market enables them to reach more potential customers than their rivals, further solidifying the advantaged position they have. In turn, these few at the top can provide more benefits and convenience to their users (think Amazon Prime) and outpace new competition before it even gets off the ground.

Although this explanation of extreme wealth and power among the big platform companies is important and cautionary, often unnoticed is how this has contributed to wealth disparity. Consider the most valuable firms in the United States—and to a large degree in the world—in 1967 and 2017: from one to five in 1967 they were IBM, AT&T, Eastman Kodak, General

Motors, and Standard Oil of New Jersey; in 2017 they were Apple, Alphabet (Google's parent), Microsoft, Amazon, and Facebook. The top five firms in 1967 created a huge number of jobs between them, both directly and indirectly through their suppliers. Not so for the five in 2017. In 1967, for example, AT&T had about one million employees. In 2017, Alphabet had only ninety-eight thousand. Software-based companies require fewer people and fewer suppliers to build wealth. As a result, only a small subset of workers can benefit from the best jobs in the most powerful companies, while large portions of the population have to compete for lower wages in less well-heeled organizations.

Regional advantage works in a similar manner.[5] In a knowledge economy, technologically oriented cities and regions with highly trained workers, entrepreneurs, and available seed capital have the lion's share of tech startups and continue to attract more companies because of their privileged position. It's remarkable that the five most valuable US companies in 2017 are headquartered in just two cities.

There is another side to regional variability. In economies with shared currency, areas that have invested and benefited the most from technology far outperform those that have been less able to invest or derive productivity gains from technology. For example, Gujarat has benefited from India's GDP growth nearly twice as much as the regions less able to take advantage of the benefits of technology.[6] Interior China, parts of the midwestern United States, and southern Europe have similar stories. This is one of the negative consequences for the EU, for example, as southern Europe has embraced technology in industry slower and lost on pricing against northern Europe. Left without intervention the trend is obvious. Wealth will accrue to fewer and fewer cities, companies, and people.

Job Losses

One of the most significant factors driving global pessimism is a numbing fear of being downsized out of the job market or forced to take low-wage positions because of new technologies. The 2019 Edelman Trust Barometer, which surveyed some thirty-three thousand people around the world, found that nearly 60 percent of respondents were worried about not having the skills to get a well-paying job in the future and 55 percent of respondents were concerned about automation or other innovations taking away their job. Richard Edelman, CEO and creator of the survey, described the attitudes beyond the numbers: "People are governed by their fears at the moment; by a two to one margin they think that the pace of innovation is too fast. Four out of five actually believe that their economic circumstances are going to be worse 10 years ahead. Those are unprecedented numbers. And it goes down to: I basically am afraid that machines are going to take my job."[7]

How realistic is this conclusion? A seminal Oxford Martin School paper published in 2013 concluded that 47 percent of US jobs are at high risk of automation in the next few decades.[8] As shown in Figure 3.1, a 2018 PwC study of twenty-nine countries found that close to 30 percent of jobs would be severely disrupted or disappear due to automation.[9] Although the precise numbers may vary, most studies agree that those hardest hit by automation will be people with lower levels of education, women, and youths.

Considering the potential scope and scale of automation technology in the future, the coming years could be extremely traumatic in the job market. Urgent responses to minimize the damage are needed. As Oxford Martin economist Carl Benedikt Frey has argued, "the Industrial Revolution created unprecedented wealth and prosperity over the long run, but the immediate consequences of mechanization were devastating for large swaths of the population. Middle-income jobs withered, wages stagnated, the labor share of income fell, profits surged, and economic inequality skyrocketed."[10] Frey suggests that these same trends are emerging during what he calls the Computer Revolution and how traumatic the consequences will be depends entirely upon how the short term is managed by helping people gain essential skills, generating new jobs, and supporting new job-creating industries or businesses during the nascent phases.

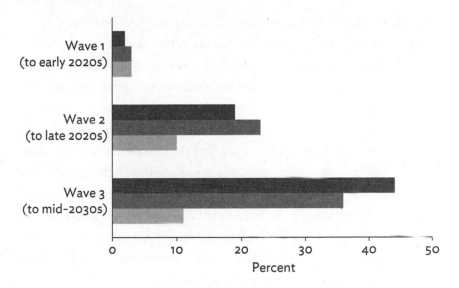

FIGURE 3.1 Percentage of existing jobs at potential risk of automation, waves.
SOURCE: PwC, "Will Robots Really Steal Our Jobs? An international analysis of the potential long term impact of automation," 2018. PwC analysis, based on data from the OECD Programme for the International Assessment of Adult Competencies public database http://www.oecd.org/skills/piaac/publicdataandanalysis/.

Privacy Intrusions

The evolution of IT platforms, cloud computing, and data analytics have resulted in amazing benefits in terms of convenience, efficiency, personalized solutions, advances in knowledge, and availability of information, products, and services. But the trade-off is that the amount of personal data stored in the cloud today exceeds all imagination. This presents a set of new challenges; critically, how do we make data available for all of the uses we find desirable while ensuring our that our privacy is safeguarded and that the data collected about us is accurate?[11]

The core issue with data accumulation and AI-based analysis of this data is that these systems need to know a lot about us—and continue to learn more and more—to generate the most accurate assessments of who we are, what we like, our hobbies, jobs, and lifestyles. More and better information about us is continuously needed to provide the personalized solutions we want technology to deliver. To be of use, the machine needs to know a lot about us. But throughout the world there is a growing backlash against technology platforms and providers that ignore people's privacy concerns. Because of this, there are increasing calls from policymakers to rein in technology companies that are less than transparent about what personal information people are giving up to use the platform and what the companies may do with this data. Most of us would find it acceptable for personal information to be used to enhance the public good, such as medical research, and to increase the quality of products or services we receive. But we are generally opposed to the loss of privacy and sense of personal security that accompanies these benefits.

Centralized Control

One of the biggest dangers of platform and other technology companies accumulating data about individuals is that this information will be in the hands of either very few, very large organizations or governments and be used for purposes not in our best interest. The platform companies have an incentive to profit from our data and governments have an incentive to use it for surveillance. The consequence of a misplaced profit motive is the subject of this chapter. As to governments and surveillance, to a degree this is already happening. For instance, the Chinese government is putting together a social scoring system that will rank every citizen using metrics such as their bill-paying history, schoolwork, adherence to traffic laws and birth control regulations, use of technology, and shopping patterns. This system will draw on information from banks, mobile phone companies, and e-commerce firms such as Alibaba, among many other sources.[12]

Less aggressive, but in some cases equally intrusive, programs in Western countries rely on data from online providers, such as Google, Apple, and mobile phone companies, for law enforcement investigations. Although these programs generally require subpoenas or warrants to access the data, there have been examples of government or law enforcement overreach. For many people, the idea that governmental authorities have channels through which to access personal data accumulated by technology companies is cause for alarm and sizably contributes to the loss of trust in public institutions.

The Disturbing Effect of Social Media

With more than two billion total users, Facebook has about as many followers as Christianity. Twitter and Instagram each have more than one hundred million active users, many of them on the platform for long periods each day. As we have seen in the many disinformation and misinformation imbroglios that these social networks have found themselves in, they have almost limitless power to distribute and distort ideas and facts, aggravate opinions and emotions, disseminate real and imagined narratives, and guide the topics that people around the globe end up talking about.

Although the social media companies should be accountable for these problematic activities on their sites, the more insidious deleterious effects of social media are a consequence of human inclinations. People spend much more time on negative content than positive content.[13] Thus not surprisingly, platform business models that depend on attracting and retaining viewers create a skew toward negative content. In addition, people are more likely to bully and demean others on social media platforms than face to face. Moreover, we tend to read things online or favor people who align with our view of the world. That, of course, solidifies the fracture of societies into idea camps that are unwilling to give credence to what others outside of their orbits have to say.

Perhaps the most dramatic criticism of social media came from Sean Parker, who founded the peer-to-peer music site Napster and advised Mark Zuckerberg when Facebook was being launched. Parker recently sold all of his Facebook holdings because of his concerns about the impact of social media platforms on society. He said that the site grew by "exploiting a vulnerability in human psychology" with people's need for attention fed by a careful reward system to keep users addicted. "We need to sort of give you a little dopamine hit every once in a while, because someone liked or commented on a photo or a post or whatever ... it's a social-validation feedback loop ... a vulnerability in human psychology," he admitted to news site *Axios*.[14]

In establishing successful platform companies, many founding entrepreneurs had noble goals of enhancing how we are governed, bringing society together, unleashing creativity and innovation, and advancing our best ideas; but this isn't happening and won't if left unmanaged.

Technology That Makes Us Dumber

University of California at San Francisco neuroscience professor Adam Gazzaley and California State University, Dominguez Hills professor of psychology Larry Rosen are concerned about smartphones and their impact on human intelligence. They describe the human brain as serving two core functions. The first, high-level thinking: synthesizing data, connecting to existing knowledge, creating, linking to emotions, planning, and deciding. The second, helping us execute plans and take action. Interestingly, our high-level cognitive functioning is well advanced beyond other species, but our critical cognitive execution capabilities—based on short-term memory and attention span—are about as good as a chimpanzee's.

That's bad enough, but in their book, aptly titled *The Distracted Mind*, Gazzaley and Rosen say that the search capacity and interruptive nature of the smartphone are worsening the situation, weakening even more our short-term intelligence. At the heart of this problem are two basic consequences of ubiquitous technology. First, we have dramatically increased our propensity to multitask, which unfortunately is really just rapidly switching from one task to another—the brain cannot really do two attentional tasks at once. Gazzaley and Rosen worry we have lost the ability to single task. "Glance around a restaurant, look at people walking on a city street, pay attention to people waiting in line for a movie or a theater, and you will see busily tapping fingers," they write. "We appear to care more about the people who are available through our devices than those who are right in front of our faces. And perhaps more critically, we appear to have the lost the ability to be simply alone with our thoughts."[15]

The second is that we have grown to spend less and less time on any single task. Our capacity to attend has shrunk—from students instructed to study a really important topic, to employees asked to work on a critical task, to driving a car. Our patience seems to be continuously shrinking: "More recent work has even suggested that the four-second rule may actually be closer to a 'two-second rule' or even a '400 millisecond rule' (less than one half a second), indicating that we are all quite impatient and prone to diverting our attention rapidly from one screen to the next if our needs are not met."[16] All of this is a result of entrancing sounds, compelling visuals, and irresistible vibrations that just cannot be ignored.

The deeper worry is that the brain is neuroplastic—it rewires itself based on use—and thus these tendencies developed early in life can sustain through our lifetime. If we read and observe in short bursts, we adapt to being able to maintain brain activity in only short bursts. If we immediately search for items we cannot remember, we let memory capacity atrophy. Certainly, technology can and does make us smarter in many ways, but the results of Gazzaley and Rosen's research point to a troubling consequence of smartphones that will only worsen if neglected.

Contributing to Self-Harm

I am extremely proud of my daughter-in-law and in the context of this chapter she probably has a job for life. Her specialty is dialectical behavior therapy, which treats people who are anxious or depressed and likely to harm themselves through cutting and suicide. We had a fascinating conversation about why self-harm is on the increase. Some of it can be credited to better reporting of patient activities and greater recognition of mental health issues. But technology plays a big role as well, she said. The reasons behind this are eye-opening.

For example, people tend to present idealized versions of themselves, their jobs, their relationships, and their family life on social media. Thus, when people who are dissatisfied with their lives or who feel inferior compare themselves to others on social media, deep depression can set in. Social media interactions can be cruel and bullying, feeding downward spirals. The Web is a hypochondriac's field of dreams. If you are not worried about a symptom now, just look it up, and you are likely to be certain you have had that symptom for some time.

Artificial Intelligence Is Puzzling

No one doubts that artificial intelligence has the potential to ultimately change our lives for the better. Supporting human intelligence with a machine that is equal in brain power will accelerate advancements in fighting diseases, developing drugs, solving engineering puzzles, managing intractable issues like climate change, freeing people from drudgery, extending creativity, distributing valuable information, and even providing companionship for the lonely and immobile.

But we don't fully understand how AI programs learn and how individual facets of AI programs affect the performance of the larger system to control outcomes sufficiently. When designing an AI program, we are still somewhat in the dark about why it does things that we did not intend it to do. What type of programming or data analysis interaction led the system to produce an unanticipated outcome? With those uncertainties, an AI system could be all too easily programmed to do something beneficial and still have the unintended consequence of causing greater harm. MIT physicist Max Tegmark provides an amusing example of this.[17] "Imagine you ask an obedient intelligent car to take you to the airport as fast as possible," he says. "It might get you there chased by helicopters and covered in vomit, doing not what you wanted but literally what you asked for." But

Tegmark is not pessimistic about the future for AI—and even our ability to effectively corral it. "We invented fire, repeatedly messed up, and then invented the fire extinguisher, fire exit, fire alarm and fire department," he reminds us.

◎ ◎ ◎

The very notion that computing technology has the potential to be our equal in intelligence presents an array of possibilities for digital devices, software, systems, and networks that go well beyond what the imagination can conjure up today. But there is an even bigger unknown: how will we handle the difficult task of crafting policies and strategies to rein in the deleterious impact of technology platforms and digitization? Especially the harm they already inflict on individual livelihoods, social relationships, the political sphere, economic systems, and global comity. To address this, we first need to fully examine the threats that technology poses from a broad and granular perspective. That knowledge alone will give us a boost in generating adequate solutions that propel technology toward being an indispensable handmaiden instead of something to worry about.

CHAPTER 4

Trust and the Crisis of Institutional Legitimacy

There are moments when you meet someone and your perspective on life changes forever. For me, that person was Jin Naibing, then the vice mayor for culture, health, and education for the city of Kunshan, in southeastern China near Shanghai. From the instant that we were introduced in 2007, Jin demonstrated an outsized understanding of global disruption— its causes, its dangers, its likely repercussions—that was astounding for someone who had never lived outside China and who had an unabashed loyalty to her relatively small city. Indeed, her particular foresight about why global institutions are failing everywhere and her clear analysis of why people distrust institutions perfectly presaged the contours of the ADAPT framework I would soon develop. Jin's analysis gave me a much more penetrating platform with which to study institutions and how they can be made to serve us better. She bemoans her own dour conclusions about institutions because, like me, Jin believes in their value (particularly the importance of great universities) in tethering towns, regions, and nations while elevating their prospects.

Now in her late fifties, she came of age in the latter stages of Mao Zedong's reign, when the Gang of Four and the Cultural Revolution were in full swing—closing universities, burning books, banishing people from the cities to work in the fields, and promoting reeducation campaigns. Although Jin hasn't spoken to me about that period, the social and political positions she has staked out for her community are the antithesis of the Cultural Revolution's tenets.

Jin's family was relatively poor when Jin was growing up. The small town of Kunshan relied on agriculture and products fired in primitive kilns for its marginal economy. But by 2003, when Jin was named Kunshan's vice mayor, the city's limited manufacturing base had been transformed into an electronics factory hub with at its peak more than four thousand, mostly Taiwanese, companies (including Foxconn, which makes Apple products). Kunshan's population had swelled, chiefly with the addition of migrants who poured into the city from rural areas in central China to work in these plants.

Jin saw the bustling economic activity in Kunshan as a golden opportunity to improve the town in crucial ways that would put it on the path toward becoming a world-class city. She believed Kunshan would be making a mistake if it assumed that its manufacturing activity would be enough to ensure a thriving future; global economic conditions change, she thought, and a city that isn't continuously taking advantage of its good fortune to make marked improvements in its residents' quality of life and social and economic prospects is in effect going backward, no matter how many factories dotted its downtown. This was not a common position for local public officials in China, either then or now; officials tend to be more conservative in their approach to enhancing local conditions, or they may use a post to advance their progress through the system, most often to another city. But Jin is unique and she has an uncommonly deep devotion to Kunshan, which grows out of a profound belief that an abiding loyalty to one's community and its people is an obligation, not merely an option.

Four of Jin's initiatives from the early 2000s are noteworthy. First, she created an education system and better housing stock for migrant workers, improving their conditions so they were on par with Kunshan's native population. Jin felt it was wrong to do otherwise. Second, she dedicated the upper story of the well-respected art museum in Kunshan to works and performances produced by the city's children, including migrants, and put on competitions to raise the profile of Kunshan's cultural output throughout the region. This effort to teach and encourage creativity among Kunshan's kids was designed to make up for the failings of China's education system and its misguided emphasis, as Jin saw it, on rote learning. It would be almost another decade before the rest of the country began to adopt new teaching strategies that more closely reflected Jin's policies in Kunshan. Third, she upgraded the quality of local healthcare facilities by seeking out private hospitals from around the world. Fourth, her most ambitious project, Jin attracted an elite American university to Kunshan.

That's what brought me to Kunshan. In 2007, just before becoming a dean at Duke University, I toured China seeking a location to establish a campus of the Fuqua School of Business. A Canadian consultant hired by Jin to help her find a university for Kunshan learned about my trip and encouraged me to meet with her. Jin's response to my introductory remarks reshaped my thinking in a profound way. In describing the reasons why she felt Kunshan needed a respected American university, Jin insightfully and deftly foreshadowed today's crisis of institutional legitimacy, which had only begun to sprout at the time.

Jin's prescient analysis of a university's value to Kunshan validated the continuing importance of institutions in the world, while simultaneously exposing the global shortcomings that lead individuals to increasingly distrust institutions and view them as irrelevant at best and malevolent at worst. Years before my conversations with people in myriad regions about their deepest worries, Jin had the uncanny sagacity to begin to sketch out the categories of the ADAPT framework—the pronounced concerns that people everywhere had—which would grow out of those exchanges. Jin's argument was so compelling and fresh that I came bearing an American business school for her city and she ended up getting an entire first-class university, dubbed Duke Kunshan.

The crux of Jin's argument about institutional failure grew out of her farsightedness concerning four troubling developments:

1. *The negative consequences of disruption.* Technological disruption would soon have a devastating effect on Kunshan and other midtier cities in developing nations. The economic success of Kunshan and its ilk was based on a low-cost, high-skilled labor model that was about to become less desirable as artificial intelligence and robotics took jobs away from local workers. (Indeed, in 2016, Foxconn cut its Kunshan workforce in half from 110,000 to 50,000, due to the introduction of robots and as many as six hundred major Kunshan companies say they have similar plans). Jin was rightfully worried that the new wave of technology would concentrate in larger cities with major universities, access to capital, and a technology-savvy employee pool, cities like Shanghai, Shenzhen, and Beijing. Not only would technological disruption destroy the economic pillars of places like Kunshan, it would also turn their residents into second-class citizens, with all of their towns' growth and progress over the recent decades overlooked and their prospects slipping.

   From an institutional perspective, Jin knew that the existing institutions in Kunshan, established to support a large, human-intensive industrial model, would require a complete overhaul for the city to maintain its prominence against other, more dominant urban areas in China, particularly as disruption changes the social and economic landscape. Kunshan would need a comprehensive strategy to install new infrastructure; attract more technologically-savvy talent, venture capitalists, and entrepreneurs who would start up new businesses and industries; retool and upgrade the existing population's skills; and build a truly smart city. To do this, Jin concluded, and not become another forgotten locale, Kunshan needed a world-class, twenty-first-century university to build around.

2. *The negative consequences of global fracturing.* Jin and I were both admirers of Samuel P. Huntington's book *The Clash of Civilizations,* in which the author argues that in the post–Cold War era, deeply embedded cultural (and in some cases religious) identity would determine the seats of

conflict in the world.[1] In this telling, China and the United States would, among other regions, vie for economic and political power based on very different cultural views of political, social, and civic structure. The risk was that this fracturing would lead to a very unstable world fraught with risks without the international institutions to manage it. As the world fractures in this way, Jin believed that institutions that could cross borders would be desperately needed to allow debate, seek agreement, and understand the comparative strengths and weaknesses among countries. She hoped that Duke, with its history of encouraging and protecting open dialogue, would fulfill that role in China, allowing for collegial and candid conversations where otherwise they were necessarily inhibited. At the same time, Jin anticipated that American students attending the university would get a more balanced and accurate picture of Chinese life, customs, beliefs, and politics than if they attended a school in the United States. In short, Jin's goal was to develop generations of young people who had a deep appreciation for the differences between the world's major societies and a respect for those distinctions.

3. *The negative consequences of demography.* Jin's third thought was targeted more at why Duke would want to set up shop in Kunshan, rather than at the reason Kunshan needed Duke. She pointed out that demography was going to put great pressure on education systems around the world. In the United States, Europe, Canada, and Australia, populations were aging and the number of domestic students applying to universities in these countries was declining. Hence, universities in these countries had become dependent on foreign student enrollment to pay the bills. Jin believed that this strategy would ultimately fail. As education systems improve in other countries and as nationalism takes hold, there would be fewer foreign students available to these schools. Opening a campus in China, one of the world's most populous countries and an attractive destination for students from around the globe, would help mitigate impending student shortages for a large university, Jin said. She was

actually making a much larger point about the impact of demography on all of our rickety institutions. Education systems have too few or too many people. Taxes increasingly depend upon diminishing population pools to provide revenue for basic services and social systems. Public job development programs and the private sector are unable to keep up with demand for good-paying positions in places where the number of young people is exploding.

4. *Institutional inertia.* Perhaps most important, as a close observer of institutions, Jin recognized that the Chinese education system as currently structured would resist the types of change needed for China to compete in a world being transformed by new technological advances. The existing system still had many elements of the Soviet educational approach it was modeled on, in which universities were generally expected to graduate students who could be put to work at state-owned enterprises, in heavy manufacturing, or at some government leaders' pet projects. In general, these activities were heavily influenced by the past—not by a future that will bear very little similarity to previous generations.

For China's educational system to respond effectively to the forces of global disruption, Jin foresaw that it would have to change radically both in terms of what was taught and researched and how it was taught and researched. It would have to be well-suited to training students for careers in private entrepreneurship, technology, and service businesses, with a focus on rapidly evolving areas of specialty such as healthcare, analytics, the environment, and new forms of biology and material science. Jin hoped to bring Duke in as a catalyst for Chinese universities, compelling them by example to adapt and provide Chinese students with the knowledge and tools they would need to navigate and innovate in a world of new dynamic technologies. Fortunately for Jin, the Chinese deputy minister of education responsible for the regulation of foreign universities agreed with her on the need for such an outside stimulus. Duke's agreement with China includes a variety of governance rules to ensure that the university's academic standards and freedoms are no different in China than in the United States. Duke was meant to be an exception that informed the whole.

Jin's insights about institutions and detrimental global trends are all the more remarkable when you consider that they came before the economic crash would worsen the fissures in the world, before the rise of neopopulist movements, before the rapid growth in disparity that marked the past ten years, before the unraveling of a consensus focused on initiatives designed to serve the global good, before the emergence of US–China tensions, before trade wars, and before the aging of China's and America's populations highlighted the threats of demographics. By pointing to the way institutions, such as a university, can serve a valuable public good that goes well beyond merely offering a degree, Jin was also challenging institutions to be dynamic and responsive to changing trends and conditions—to safeguard traditional civic norms and to be sufficiently malleable to reshape their own roles for the better as norms shift.

Unfortunately, Jin's worst fears about global institutional sclerosis have been borne out. In different ways all institutions that are designed to make our societies work are in crisis—the international order, most political systems, health systems, financial systems, legal and policing systems, tax systems, and the fourth estate. The most direct evidence of this crisis was captured by the 2020 Edelman Trust Barometer (Figure 4.1). In this survey, which measured attitudes toward institutions and social and political systems in twenty-six countries, less than one person in five said that the system is working for them and nearly three-quarters of respondents expressed a sense of injustice about the world they live in and a desire for change.

Institutions are struggling to navigate a contradiction. Typically, being slow to adapt is a plus for institutions central to the effective functioning of society. Without a stable police force, for example, we do not have security. Without a stable financial system, organizations, products, and services cannot get formulated and built, and business cannot be conducted. Without a stable tax system, governments do not have the money to run

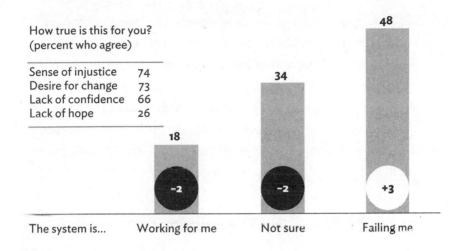

FIGURE 4.1 Percentage of population who feel that the system is working for them. SOURCE: 2020 Edelman Trust Barometer.

themselves. Without a stable education system, the population cannot learn, grow, and adapt. Traditionally, we trust and rely on institutions because they in fact provide stability.

But in a time of severe technological disruption, economic uncertainty, cynical political disinformation campaigns, racial and social fracturing, questions being raised about whether schools are providing the type of education that students need and mounting worries among so many people that the system as a whole is leaving them behind, institutions must be more agile and adapt to help minimize the harm that these and other trends can inflict. How long can political discourse be infected by false information on social media before democracy and fair elections are permanently undermined? Can police forces defy calls for more transparency when communities, rightly or wrongly, believe they are under siege from the police themselves, their presumed protectors?

The challenge for institutions is for them to be able to change rapidly without inciting insecurity in the society they are designed to serve and without damaging the essential oversight that makes them stable forces in the world. If institutions change too fast, or in the wrong way, they risk disenfranchising the people they are designed to serve. However, if they change too slowly, they risk irrelevance. To examine this difficult balancing act more closely—and, really, the inability of institutions to manage it well—it is useful to more closely analyze how institutional failure in an age of disruption is playing out through the lens of essential institutions in our societies.

Technological Disruption: The Erosion of the Fourth Estate

Without real intervention, existing critical institutions are either maladaptive to a technology-based world or undermined by it. Consider the plight of the media, which we touched on in chapter 1. Complaints about the accuracy of the press have always been with us, but at least since colonial times and the rise in influence of institutionalists like Edmund Burke it was generally accepted that the press's essential role in society was to help ensure an informed citizenry.[2] Without an informed populace, democracy cannot thrive, because under that system people have to make decisions about the future of their countries—and without accurate information, they cannot make good choices. The problem is, many people don't believe any more that the media is an honest broker. For instance, according to a Pew Foundation survey in the United States, 46 percent more Democrats than Republicans believe that the press acts in the interest of the public. Even more alarming, only 16 percent of Republicans highly engaged in the news trust what the press produces, compared with 91 percent of Democrats.[3]

In other words, the press today is seen as serving the public good by only half of the population—and politically a very specific half. Similar results emerge from surveys in Europe with trust in press at the lowest point among people who consider themselves middle class and residents of southern European countries that are not performing as well as their northern counterparts. Finally, throughout the world people who do not support their current governments are more likely to feel that the media is not covering political issues fairly.

With these survey results, it should come as little surprise that twelve of the top fifteen polarizing brands in the United States are media companies, according to Morning Consult.[4] Trump Hotels, Smith and Wesson, and Nike are the sole nonmedia organizations on that list. I suspect everyone can predict the two media firms that are most polarizing: CNN and Fox News. Living in the United States and being unable to avoid seeing what is on these two stations from time to time, it is easy to conclude that some parts of the media are indeed extremely tilted. I have had dozens of conversations with people who have expressed concerns that competing views of politics are causing conflict in their families, among spouses, parents, children, and siblings. When I ask them where they get their news and information, it is clear that they are starting from completely different bases of fact—invariably one watches Fox News and the other CNN. I usually suggest they find a more neutral source they can agree on as a starting point for their discussions. Most cannot find one.[5] It is naïve to believe that media was ever really "neutral" in the absolute sense of the word, but journalistic balance in reporting and lack of bias in presenting a story seem to be disappearing at an alarming rate.

The combination of three interwoven elements best explain press polarization. First is the general loosening of regulations that require media to be balanced in its coverage. Second, there are so many more news options across the political spectrum to choose from as lower barriers to entry create dozens of new information channels on the Web, TV, radio, and podcasts. Third are commercial opportunities. In the scramble among new and existing news organizations for profitability, the winners are media organizations that can attract a large audience cohort from the vast disintermediated group of eyeballs and ears seeking information. In that environment, finding and maintaining a large following is difficult without a compelling and hard-to-resist sales pitch. As it turns out, the most irresistible option for people are echo chambers that confirm their political beliefs rather than oblige them to question their version of the truth.

Global Fracturing: The Decay of Multilateral Institutions

Budding national insularity—countries digging in to defend social, cultural, and political differences rather than endeavoring to forge compromise across differences—splinters the world into dozens of separate, unyielding parts. This causes a more profound issue: fracturing is depriving us of the cooperative global institutions we need to address problems at an international level. This splintering is undoubtedly under way now. For instance, meetings such as the G7 and G20 once played a valuable part in providing nations with informal means to help steer through challenging issues across the globe. This was on full display in 2007–2008, when the G20 finance ministers used the goodwill and consensus of their group to right the global financial system after the market crash. Lately, however, G-level meetings have become less effective as countries and leaders pursue their own self-interest over seeking a collective global agenda, be it on climate change, trade, or any other pressing issue.[6] In many ways the G-summits have abetted the rise of populism, nationalism, and political polarization and have been decreasingly successful because of that.

But the G20 is not the only significant multilateral institution that is on the ropes today. In 2016, South Africa withdrew from the International Criminal Court, a twenty-year-old organization formed to prosecute international transgressions, including genocide and war crimes. Burundi, The Gambia, and Russia soon followed. The World Trade Organization has been unable to agree on its latest liberalization of global trades rules, known as the Doha Development Agenda, an effort that has been under way for two decades. And perhaps the most prominent illustration: in 2019 in the UK, the Conservative Party won a decisive victory in the General Election on a clear anti-EU platform that ended three years of uncertainty and accelerated the government's plan to take the UK out of the EU. These are just a few examples, as the list is indeed very long.

Since multilateral institutions are voluntary, there are two primary requirements for them to be successful: all parties must abide by their decisions and they should appear to perform the functions they were designed for.[7] Neither of those requirements hold very often anymore. Only two countries are abiding by the Paris Climate Accord; there were two more vetoes in the UN Security Council in the past five years than in the entire decade from 1990 to 2000 and were only two less than there were between 2000 to 2010. A host of countries are completely ignoring the Nuclear Non-proliferation Treaty.

Polarization makes sustaining multilateral institutions increasingly difficult, as national leaders are focused on the particular interests of their own country to the exclusion of broader global interests. What is most disturbing is that there are still issues at a global scale that require engaged coordinated action, such as climate change, management of infectious diseases, nuclear proliferation, military conflicts, and elements of trade and job growth. Without effective multilateral organizations, these issues will not be resolved.

Demographic Dilemma: The Shortcomings of Education

Demographic trends are seriously impacting educational systems. In more economically developed countries, where population growth has slowed, there is less revenue available to improve educational opportunities, in part because tax receipts and the number of applicants are in decline. And in generally less well-heeled countries, where the cohort of young people as a percentage of the population is skyrocketing, the need for stellar educational programs starting from elementary school could not be more urgent, but the financial wherewithal and the ability to develop these programs are lacking.

In truth, educational systems as indispensable institutions have failed us for quite some time; the consequences are just more perilous today. For instance, most of the best precollege private schools and universities are off-limits to less wealthy people unless the student can fight through the chain of obstacles that stand in the way of good scholarships. This advantage for richer families continues in the graduate school realm: the universities providing the greatest opportunities after graduation dispro-portionately admit wealthy students. All of this produces a vicious cycle in which wealth provides access to better education and improves education outcomes.[8] This often leads to more wealth and more educational oppor-tunities for the next generation of the top 1 percent families.

To interrupt this cycle, sufficient funding of public education at the ele-mentary to high school and university levels is required. That, however, is nearly impossible today. Part of the problem is another flagging institution: tax systems. The current forms and levels of taxation are leading to sharp reductions in the overall amount of money available for critical social needs like education. In most countries today, tax policies tend to favor the rich, deriving proportionately less money from the top 1 percent than the rest of the population. This is in sharp contrast to tax-paying ratios of the mid-twentieth century and is worsening along with income disparity.

Equally problematic, sales or value-added tax (VAT) are a larger burden for those on the lower rungs of the economic ladder because poorer people spend a higher percentage of their wealth than their richer counterparts. Property taxes also tilt toward the wealthy, who typically own valuable property, but relative to their overall wealth, any one piece of real estate is proportionately less of their total assets than for the typical homeowner.

By depending so heavily on the lower economic strata to cover rev-enue needs, governments at all levels are setting themselves up for cash flow shortfalls. In fact, since 2000, tax revenue as a percentage of GDP has declined in Australia, Canada, Denmark, Finland, Ireland, Israel, Norway, Sweden, and the United States.[9] With less money in government coffers, education and other social needs like infrastructure improvements or upskilling job training are by necessity starved. Regressive tax systems—in name or in actuality—ultimately pit the rich against the poor, creating a resentment gap between people who have the money to pay for whatever they need and less wealthy people who are unable to save to cover, say, college tuition. In the context of education, fewer tax receipts results in inadequate schools, which turn out graduates who are ill-prepared to contribute to technological innovation, organizational breakthroughs, and cultural creativity that are needed to juice economic growth. As the economy ebbs, tax yields fall in concert.

Without sufficient tax revenue to fund public universities, an alternative is to raise tuition at these schools. But that is not a viable option anymore, in part because of the demographic crisis. This is particularly true in Western countries where the population is aging and thus the number of domestic students is declining. Increasing prices is obviously not an answer to falling demand. With the deeper international relationships formed by globalization slowly fracturing, fewer overseas students are applying to nondomestic schools; indeed, some of them are restricted from doing so by immigration policies promulgated by nationalist governments. Perhaps most important, raising public university tuition may not be a good idea under any circumstances: it harms the students these schools are most intended to help get an education as the least well-off enrollees are either shut out by higher costs or have to incur high amounts of debt to pay their way through school, leaving them further behind upon graduation.

Finally, universities could potentially solve some of the revenue shortfall by developing programs that target the lifelong learning needs of adults, especially in a period of technological disruption when reskilling is an imperative for many. But few schools have even begun to consider this potential group of students and big institutions are slow to change; the exceptions are the few fortunate enough to have leaders like Jin Naibing to put themselves on the line in the service of radical transformation.

◉ ◉ ◉

When functioning well, our institutions make us stronger; they provide the social goods and essential services that make society work. And they are at risk. If they were businesses, we could simply let them fail to eventually be replaced by something else. The problem is they are critical elements of society that provide the basic fabric that makes things work. Thus their potential failure, or even significant performance problems, is a crisis for society that needs to be addressed across a broad swath of our institutions by the people responsible for those institutions at the local, regional, and national levels. We only miss the glue that holds things together when it is gone. When we really notice institutions are not working, it may be too late.

CHAPTER 5

Polarization and the Crisis of Leadership

I have spent much of my professional life helping to prepare leaders. My current role includes both strategy and leadership development and previously I founded and led Duke Corporate Education, which has been considered one of the best in the world at executive education. Yet, if you think about the thematic threads of this book, it seems that all of us in the business of developing the next generation of leaders have failed. We erred by overlooking the possibility that globalization could have serious side effects and that the new global order was in part a chimera and destined to be short-lived. We ignored the prospect that because of these side effects— really, unanticipated consequences—the next generation of leaders would face a world that is much different and, in countless ways, more difficult to steer through than previous generations did.

Of the five elements in the ADAPT framework (asymmetry, disruption, age, polarization, and trust), polarization impacts leadership the most. In ADAPT's taxonomy "polarization" is meant as a summary term for three closely related phenomena that result from fracturing and rejection of the status quo at different levels of society: a breakdown in global consensus as well as rising nationalism and mounting populism and divisiveness within countries and regions. These three factors have essentially neutered global institutions that had been vehicles for collaborative solutions to big global problems. Simultaneously they have led to the ascendance of contentious politics based on blinkered parochialism and gaslighting. Spearheads of some populist movements maintain their power by convincing constituents that the rest of the world—indeed anybody who disagrees with them at home—are both not worthy of attention and intent on destroying their ways of life. Some of the leaders with more of a globalist bent dismiss the very legitimate concerns of the many individuals who have given up on optimism for a better future.

In this hardened environment, only a few leaders have been able to eclipse polarization and its consequent cynicism and make a meaningful impact. They perceive their role as enriching lives and living conditions wherever they have influence and inspiring people to elevate themselves and their interactions with others through collaboration, integrity, honesty, and ethical behavior. By contrast, most other would-be leaders, though perhaps armed with the best intentions, are hampered by an obsolete playbook written in the heyday of globalization. This means that we who believe that great managers of ideas, people, companies, and politics are indispensable for the world to overcome its perilous shortcomings by 2030 have a larger task at hand than ever before: we must develop new types of leaders who are strategically innovative and politically sophisticated and who possess rare combinations of human attributes—such as heroism and humility or a locally rooted, globally sculpted worldview (more on these and other leadership attributes in chapter 12).

The crisis of leadership spawned by polarization has effectively paralyzed the world, keeping us from addressing the most crucial issues that threaten our future at home or abroad. The best way to see how close to the bone the leadership implications of polarization are is through the lens of the second major disruption due to the ubiquitous use of technology: climate change. There is near consensus among scientists that, left unabated, climate change will result in drastic consequences, ranging from elimination of a vast number of species, meaningful harm to the ocean and reef life in particular, rising water levels drowning many low-lying coastal areas, as well as extreme weather and severe drought resulting in crop loss

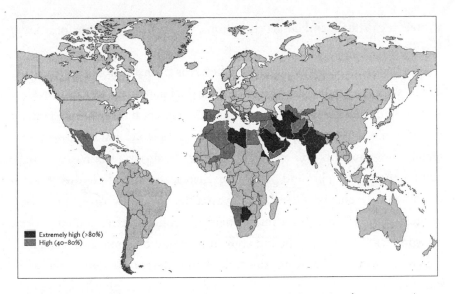

MAP 5.1 Projected water scarcity in 2025. SOURCE: WRI Aqueduct (www.wri.org/aqueduct; accessed on January 29, 2020). Redrawn by Bill Nelson

and deforestation.[1] Most scientists also agree that, if we do not address climate issues within the next decade, many of the consequences will be irreversible and we risk accelerating dangerous natural processes, such as the release of methane from the Arctic. That would add a much more aggressive heat-trapping gas into the atmosphere.[2]

As with the other crises detailed in this book, climate change exacerbates all of the elements of ADAPT. The crisis of prosperity is inflamed because the world's least wealthy regions and the least well-off people in any country are the most impacted by it. Equatorial regions will experience the greatest drought effects. Some of the world's poorest countries are extremely low-lying. Less well-built homes bear the brunt of the damage from hurricanes and tornadoes. Of course, this is not by accident; the richest individuals within a society and the most powerful people have chosen the most arable, hospitable, and protected lands for themselves. In addition, the well-heeled have the wherewithal to flee areas that are subject to creeping drought and desert conditions, while the poorest are forced to stay (Map 5.1).

The impact of climate change on the crisis of institutional legitimacy can be seen in a number of areas. Consider the financial system. Insurance will be under tremendous strain. Mortgage lenders have not sufficiently priced in massive loan defaults that may occur due to climate and weather effects. Governments will experience greater strain on resources as a result of emergency relief and population displacement and the disruption due to climate change. Given the devastating, comprehensive, and even existential threat posed by climate change, a collaborative, unified effort by world leaders to confront and combat it should be uncontroversial. As we know, however, that is not the case. Four different by-products of polarization stand in the way of enlightened and effective global leadership on this issue:

1. The rejection of expertise;

2. Polarization of fact bases;

3. Polarization of priorities;

4. Nationalism and the breakdown of global consensus.

The Rejection of Expertise

Despite the overwhelming scientific evidence generated by hundreds of carefully drawn studies that climate change is real and its dangers are not to be trifled with, large groups of people across the world deny these conclusions. This is a direct result of polarization, which encourages people of one stripe to reject experts no matter how grounded in facts and data they are, when the other side supports the assertions of these experts.

In the case of climate change, individuals with a particular political bent tend to dismiss it, but broadly speaking confirmation bias is prevalent on both sides of the political spectrum these days. Or, as media and communications scholar Erik Nisbet and his colleagues at Ohio State found in a wide-ranging study, "liberals and conservatives alike react negatively to dissonant science communication, resulting in diminished trust of the scientific community."[3] For instance, try to get a progressive person in the United States to acknowledge that Walmart singlehandedly led a huge energy savings campaign by using its retail power to switch consumers from incandescent light bulbs to LEDs. Even presented with the facts—80 percent fewer greenhouse gases per light bulb—left-leaning people have told me that "Walmart probably paid somebody off to say that; everything they do destroys the environment."

Others, like Greg Lukianoff and Jonathan Haidt in their book, *The Coddling of the American Mind*, point to the movement on campuses to eliminate words and ideas that may be disturbing to some students—in today's terminology, erecting safe spaces—as another enabler of confirmation bias.[4] If certain concepts or positions can be deemed wrong by definition, how can we expect people to listen to what others with different opinions say and reach broader agreement on facts through dialogue while appreciating the value of expertise, even if the conclusion is discomforting?

Polarization of Fact Bases

Social media is a big culprit in the polarization of facts. These echo chambers allow people to read information supportive of their own beliefs—it is spoon-fed to them by content preference algorithms, often not filtered or fact-checked—thus enhancing their distrust of experts who argue anything that doesn't align with what was dispensed on social media.

Lukianoff and Haidt say that all of this is part of a generally held tendency today that life is a battle between good people and bad people. In American political parlance this makes it difficult to cross the aisle, because those who hold conflicting views are by definition "bad." Solving climate change issues is going to require a lot of very difficult trade-offs, but how can a leader even begin to start a discussion about these trade-offs if even mentioning them will likely result in being seen as part of the "other" camp and hence immediately discounted?

Polarization of Priorities

I was in Paris early in 2019 after President Emmanuel Macron had raised gas prices by a small amount and all hell broke loose. Activists known as the Gilets Jaunes hit the streets, angrily demanding that Macron roll back the increase; in the end, they won. I suspect that will be commonplace as we try to tackle climate issues. Indeed, the Gilets Jaunes and their supporters had perfectly legitimate reasons to complain. Housing prices in Paris, like many major cities, have become prohibitively expensive. The result is that people who do what many of us would call real work—repair things, serve food, manage cash registers, among other jobs—have to travel well outside of the city to find a reasonable place to live. They must be able to afford the commute to Paris. Even a small rise in gasoline prices can break such a fragile budget.

Almost everything we need to do to address climate may produce similarly problematic outcomes, if only in the short term. Invariably these outcomes will intensify other issues. Wealth disparity will grow as the transition costs to new forms of energy are absorbed by those least well-off; disruption will increase as jobs in the energy industry are shifted toward producing less carbon-intensive fuels; countries with older populations will incur additional burdens on their already tapped-out national revenue bases as fuel taxes will phase out; and countries with large groups of young people will have to find ways to create jobs without following the growth strategies that every other country in the world implemented—that is, using inexpensive energy to support rapid industrialization.

In today's polarized global environment, people view their priorities as sacrosanct, which brooks no compromise. Battle lines are drawn almost immediately and everyone believes that they are feeling the most pain when a trade-off is presented. Everyone rejects the notion that some sacrifice and collaboration to craft solutions with neighbors close and far are necessary when confronting an existential threat like climate change. The challenge for the leader attempting to deal with climate change is not just how to address those costs but that people have extremely different views on their relative priority.

Nationalism and the Breakdown of Global Consensus

It is instructive to look at the number of international groups that have proclaimed climate change to be an emergency—everyone from mayors around the world to a host of UN agencies to dozens of global science organizations and NGOs. However, none of these groups alone, or even collectively, have the capacity to do much about climate change. In the end, only nation-states can address this problem by introducing appropriate regulation—for example, setting limits on their greenhouse activities.

The 2016 Paris climate accord was a first step in this direction because it set climate change targets for each nation. However, these are voluntary goals and would not have been approved if the targets were compulsory. Very few countries that signed the accord are living up to its objectives. Only Morocco and The Gambia have kept temperature increases to 1.5 degrees centigrade above preindustrial levels and five more have limited increases to 2 degrees centigrade.[5] (The overall goal of the Paris Agreement is to hold global average temperature increases to "well below 2 degrees centigrade above preindustrial levels.") None of these seven countries are major contributors to greenhouse gases.

There are two key challenges in achieving the targets set out in Paris, both having to do with growing nationalist tendencies. First, worsening economic and political tensions among nations makes peer pressure a decreasingly effective strategy. For example, how can China or France convince the United States to change its mind about leaving the Paris Agreement when the United States is in a trade war with both nations? Second, the Paris Agreement has elements of the "tragedy of the commons" first identified by economist William Lloyd in the nineteenth century. Lloyd argued that individuals or groups of individuals act in their own self-interest at the expense of the common good by depleting shared resources.[6]

It is in everyone's interest globally that the climate crisis be mitigated. But that will come at a cost; hence, there is an incentive for each country to set a low target and imperfectly follow through on that target. In a time of growing nationalism and political and economic competition among nations, the desire to cheat, exhibit selfish tendencies, and pad one's own pockets is much greater than in periods of economic and political interdependence. Why would any country in this polarized environment want to agree to a compulsory global climate accord when it has local self-centered reasons not to? Brazil's economic difficulties provide a natural justification for farmers to burn the rainforest; Southeast Asia's growth is primarily fueled by carbon-based energy sources; US energy independence is based on inexpensive oil and gas from greenhouse gas–intensive fracking; Australia, Canada, Russia, and Saudi Arabia depend on oil to power their economies; and China can convert its economy only so fast from a carbon-dependent energy system.

◎ ◎ ◎

Most leaders attempting to take on urgent issues, including climate change, begin with a baleful trust deficit. In this polarized landscape—when the other side may be deemed evil before uttering a word—the lack of trust is frequently not expressed cordially, to put it mildly. The boiling passions and nasty words, as well as the deviance of dishonest opposition research that disseminates real or fake information about potential leaders' private lives, only makes the path toward great leadership even more pocked with landmines. Thus, while the worst consequences of polarization have forged a crisis of leadership, they also have made the idea of becoming a leader much less desirable. So although the crisis of leadership is primarily about the challenge of leading today, an equally important question is, Who will have the courage to take the job?

CHAPTER 6

Age, Accelerating the Four Crises

First impressions upon landing in India are vivid. You are surprised by the diversity of vehicles and animals sharing the road, sometimes oxen and elephants with hordes of bicycles, motorbikes, three-wheel taxis, cars, trucks, and buses. But it is the pedestrians who approach you at the stoplights you notice most. The first time you see the deep brown, sad eyes of a girl in a tattered dress tapping on your car window, asking for any change you can spare, creates an indelible memory. You are struck by the dust on her dress, shoes, and hair, causing you to see the dust everywhere and realize you are sharing a two-lane road with six lanes of traffic. You are confronted by the number of people on bicycles or motorbikes who are in their twenties. They seem never to stop. How could the world have so many twenty-year-olds all in this one place?

The experience in Japan is quite different. If you are in a car, it may be the cleanest you have ever sat in, the driver has white gloves with no dirt apparent, and the roads are immaculate, wide and seemingly empty of people. If you have just arrived from India, your first question may be, Where are all the twenty-year-olds? Should you drive into rural areas, you may feel that you've entered a region of ghost towns; according to a 2013 Japanese government report, more than eight million properties in Japan are unoccupied, and nearly a quarter have been abandoned, meaning that they are neither for sale nor for rent.[1] Scattered among the abandoned houses are old people with forlorn expressions; the young have fled to the cities. Many of the abandoned homes are unattractive to potential buyers because they have been the sites of suicides or "lonely deaths"—seniors who have died in place and remained undiscovered for often long periods of time.[2]

Demography Accelerates the Institutional Crisis

Demographics has created a time bomb for the world and we don't have much time left on the clock to address it. The world population, which was just over three billion in 1960, has grown to just under eight billion. And these eight billion are sharply divided into two very different groups: one in countries whose populations are shrinking and aging rapidly and the other in countries that have large populations of young people. The result is a classic mismatch of resource and need. Even more important, age acts as an amplifier of the other crises, making all of them more urgent. The divide between rich and poor, both in and across nations, becomes greater. Disruption of society accelerates as labor forces and tax bases in older countries dwindle, while unemployment and unrest in younger countries grows. Young migrants seeking opportunity stoke the fires of populism among older populations. The failure of institutions to address the pressing needs of either group feeds the crisis of institutional legitimacy around the world.

At the extremes there is a more than thirty-year gap in median age between the world's oldest and youngest countries.[3] It is mind-blowing to think about a three-decade difference between the median age of given countries. There are not just a few countries on either side of this gap. There are fifty countries with a median age over forty and thirty-seven countries with a median age under twenty. That is roughly one-third of all the countries reported in the CIA's *World Factbook*. Japan is the third-oldest while India is the eighty-sixth youngest, but many of the youngest countries are in Africa. In Europe such countries as Italy and Greece are aging at an even faster rate than Japan.

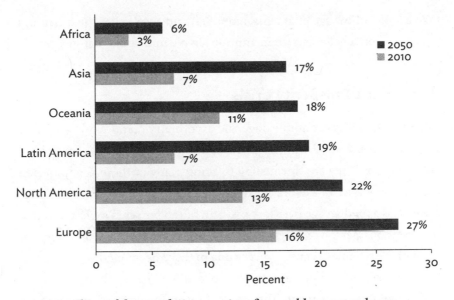

FIGURE 6.1 Share of the population age sixty-five or older, 2010 and 2050 (**percent**). NOTE: Caribbean countries are included in Latin America. SOURCE: United Nations Population Division World Population Prospects, 2012 Revision.

At the broadest level, nations like Japan are those with a rapidly growing population of elderly citizens; these countries tend to be more affluent overall and there is a well-established correlation between affluence and declining fertility rates. They enjoyed extraordinary success under the economic model much of the world adhered to for seventy years and remain wedded to that model as a solution for their problems rather than reframing their thinking for today's challenges. Conversely, young nations are less affluent and tend to have much higher fertility rates. Their leaders see the immense risks associated with a young population needing education and economic opportunity, but they have neither the funds nor the systemic vision to address these risks.

Despite the appearance of two very different worlds as shown in Figure 6.1, there is of course only one, and the problems of the youngest populations and the aging populations are a recipe for disaster for all of us. Let's take a look at how age augments, amplifies, and accelerates the crises and poses different challenges for institutions in old and young nations.

Age and the Prosperity Crisis

In developed older economies, age and asymmetry compound each other in many ways; a good way to get a sense for how massive the problems are—and how they are threatening to bring many of these economies to their knees—is to look at old age dependency ratios. Every country in Figure 6.2 has a median age over forty. A ratio of 100 percent would mean that there was one person over sixty-five for every person in the workforce. For most of the twentieth century, every one of these developed countries had a ratio of less than 25 percent, but by 2030 all will be north of 35 percent, with Japan over 50 percent. This spells disaster for these nations by 2030 unless something is done. Why? Because most of these economies have relied on those in the fifteen to sixty-five cohort to supply the labor and the consumption upon which the economies run.

At the same time, these people saved money for retirement, contributed to various public and private pension schemes, paid taxes to fund services for seniors, and directly supported their elderly relatives. The skyrocketing old age dependency ratios illustrated here have pulled the rug out from under this system. Not only is the sixty-five-plus cohort growing in number, but they're living longer too. For far too many of these senior citizens, personal savings are proving inadequate as the portion of life spent in retirement and typically in less robust health grows longer. Welfare systems and social safety nets, which these people contributed to, or at least counted on, were designed with a different set of assumptions about how many would call on those systems for support and, critically, for how long they would be dependent on them. With both savings and support systems proving inadequate to the needs of the older population, many of the elderly are falling into poverty or near-poverty.

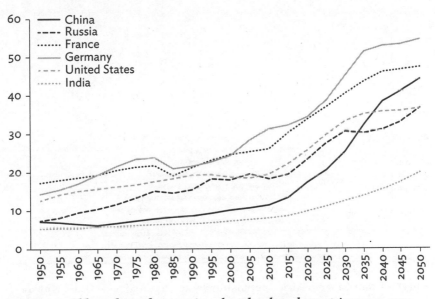

FIGURE 6.2 Old age dependency ratio, select developed countries, 1950–2050.
ɴᴏᴛᴇ. Ratio of population aged 65 per 100 population 16 64) UN Medium Variant. ꜱᴏᴜʀᴄᴇ:
United Nations, World Population Prospects: The 2017 Revision.

Meanwhile, the burden of supporting the elderly weighs on a shrinking labor force. The result is that workers are facing higher taxes paid into the system, whether they be for pension and welfare schemes or to subsidize healthcare costs; increased calls for financial help from elderly relatives; and decreased ability to put aside money for their own retirement. Affluent citizens in these economies benefit from generous retirement plans, healthy investment portfolios, and appreciating real estate values; it is these very people who tend to fill leadership positions in government and business. They are insulated from the problems most citizens face and thus don't bring the proper sense of urgency to these problems, but these pressures from an unfavorable dependency ratio are contributing to the hollowing out of the middle class. With old age dependency ratios increasing

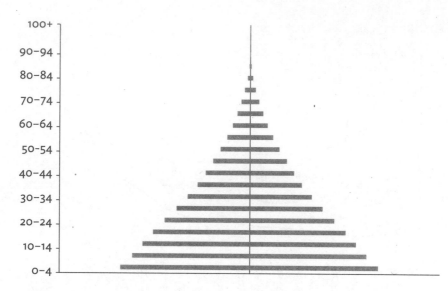

FIGURE 6.3 **Sub-Saharan Africa population by age, 2030.** SOURCE: United Nations, World Population Prospects: The 2017 Revision.

into the foreseeable future, this downward spiral will only become worse, contributing to further inequity and dysfunction.

And what of the developing economies with much younger populations? As has been mentioned and shown in Figure 6.3, Africa is home to many of the nations with the world's youngest populations. According to the 2020 CIA Factbook, there are thirty-one countries where the median age is under twenty years old.[4] Of those, twenty-eight are in Africa. By the UN's estimates, these African nations had a total population of 866 million in 2015; by 2030 that number is expected to grow to 1.29 billion, of which 261 million will be between the ages of fifteen and twenty-four. This represents a huge number of people who will be in need of education or meaningful employment. By UN estimates, in 2030, Nigeria alone will have nearly 54 million people in the fifteen to twenty-four age cohort, while Kenya will have more than 13 million. In part, this enormous challenge is due to what most people would consider to be good news: childhood mortality in Africa has dropped precipitously in recent decades, as it has in much of the world.

In the past, these nations might look to developed economies to provide aid in the form of funding or loans, but with developed nations increasingly beset by the age-driven or age-exacerbated problems described above, help may be less likely. Among those developed nations that see it in the interest of the global economy to help any way they can, the sheer size of the problem is daunting at best and insurmountable at worst.

Age and Institutional Disruption

Younger developing nations like those in Africa are likely to be deprived of what has been a stepping-stone to establishing a middle class in the late twentieth century: labor arbitrage. As a true global economy developed after World War II, industrial corporations from developed countries found that they could lower the largest component of manufacturing (labor costs) by setting up locations in countries with low labor rates. This phenomenon had obvious benefits for the home country but also provided important sources of employment in younger developing nations. These enterprises gave local workers the opportunity to learn and copy. Taiwan and South Korea, to name but two examples, grew rich by following their "workshop of the world" strategies. However, as artificial intelligence and robotics sweep the manufacturing sectors of most developed nations, this well-trodden road to bolstering a middle class may be disappearing, leaving nations like those mentioned in Africa, as well as populous, youthful nations like Indonesia, with fewer options at the very time when more are needed because of their growing youth population.

Moreover, economies that have made some progress already providing offshore labor to the developed world are seeing erosion of jobs in those sectors. For example, if we look at who is most likely to be affected in India's highly lucrative IT outsourcing business, it will be the least skilled and thus those least able to find other work. Over the next decade we'll see robots doing the entire job of some skilled workers as well.

If technology has disrupted business models and industries around the world, age is an equally potent disrupter of institutions, infrastructure, and societal norms. In developing economies, where educational systems have often struggled to make a notable difference in terms of employment readiness to even a small slice of the population, the huge increase in young people brought about by declining childhood mortality rates and fewer instances of extreme poverty now takes the form of a tsunami threatening to swamp all in its path. Even those who have worked hard to improve literacy will struggle to keep up. In Indonesia, the world's fourth most populous country, where the median age hovers around thirty, twelve years of education are compulsory, yet most of the population is functionally illiterate. India, soon to be the most populous nation on earth, believes it will need to build more than half a million new schools by 2030.[5] It's easy to see that the cost of infrastructure required by these burgeoning young population cohorts is immense. Across the developing world, young people are streaming into cities that were built for much smaller populations. The consequences of not meeting these needs are high unemployment, depressed economic growth, social unrest, and increased emigration—especially of the best and the brightest.

In older developed nations, age is equally disruptive but in different ways. First, automation in the workplace threatens to further undermine the ability of the labor force to carry its senior citizens. PwC has estimated that developed nations may have anywhere from 20 percent to just under 40 percent of current jobs at risk of automation in the next fifteen years. Of course, new jobs will be created as well, but the biggest question will be whether those who have lost jobs to robots and AI will have the skills to fill the new positions. In any event, significant job loss will result and those displaced by automation will find themselves competing for social safety net funding with the burgeoning elderly population—at the same time that those funds are put under greater pressure because of a diminished tax base. The aging tax base threatens to squeeze funds for infrastructure investment in older nations, where in many cases the need is enormous; many developed nations, including the United States, are faced with crumbling cities, roads, and bridges built for a different time. According to the Council on Foreign Relations, the American Society of Civil Engineers has estimated that the total infrastructure gap in the United States will reach $1.5 trillion by 2025.[6]

Meanwhile, the healthcare systems in many older countries are already struggling to handle the growing legions of retirees. Healthcare costs per capita are skyrocketing throughout the developed world; the ten largest OECD members have seen this figure in United States purchasing power parity (PPP) dollars increase more than 160 percent over the past two decades.[7] The growing healthcare sectors in these countries are of course a source of employment for those displaced by automation elsewhere, but pay is often lower than what could have been earned on the factory floor.

◎ ◎ ◎

Clearly, the challenges outlined in the first part of the book are enormous and seem too overwhelming to successfully corral. If we try to employ answers copied directly from those who guided us in the post–World War II period, we will be relegated to watching or, worse, participating in exacerbating our problems and cause irreversible harm. A better approach—an imperative one—is to adapt the underlying ideas from the model that helped generate so much success to address their unintended consequences. Exploring those new solutions is the job of Part 2 of the book.

PART II
CONQUERING THE CRISES

IN THE BOOK'S INTRODUCTION I OUTLINED THE CAUSES OF THE
ADAPT crises, examined throughout Part 1. The generally accepted model
(Figure P2.1) that guided global revival and an era of remarkable growth
nearly everywhere after World War II is no longer fit for purpose. Although
once a positive force, this model is now revealing its dark side.

To be sure, this model and the institutions that supported it connected
the world in unprecedented ways, created extraordinary economic gains,
and brought many people out of poverty. But as the world changed, without
notable reassessment or attempts to curb their least effective and harmful
unintended consequences, this approach produced measurable disparities
and ushered in a winner-take-all world, put jobs at risk, weakened communities and social compacts, split us apart, and produced an environmentally
unsustainable model. ADAPT and its associated crises grew directly out of
our overreliance on this worldview for more than seventy years.

A number of radical solutions have been offered to mitigate the negative
ramifications of this model: dismantle it, eliminate capitalism altogether,
build walls and strangle trade, or replace business, markets, and institutions with entirely new structures. These ideas are by and large not fully
thought out and would be foolhardy to adopt for a variety of reasons, but
none more persuasive than that elements of the postwar change model are
essential to continued success; many of its interconnected elements need

FIGURE P2.1 The shared global alignment that drove success following World War II. SOURCE: Created by the authors.

rethinking. Consequently, each facet of the old model needs to be reevaluated and modified to better address and reflect today's conditions and needs. One goal here is to describe what this new model and the change process to achieve it might look like (Figure P2.2).

The individual but intertwined elements of this revised model, which contains the same elements as its predecessor but has been rethought, are explored in some depth in chapters 7–10, which offer solutions to propel a more equitable, inclusive, and prosperous world. Sometimes these solutions are spelled out through argument, but most often by looking at the efforts of creative and resourceful people who are spearheading innovative ideas and programs targeted at the problems identified earlier in the book. As a group, these chapters show that we need to revisit the core assumptions that drove the past seventy years and reimagine our institutions and shared culture to support new sets of ideas.

Chapter 7: Strategy: Rethinking Economic Growth—Local First

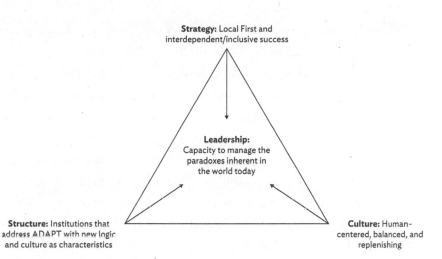

Strategy: Local First and interdependent/inclusive success

Leadership: Capacity to manage the paradoxes inherent in the world today

Structure: Institutions that address ADAPT with new logic and culture as characteristics

Culture: Human-centered, balanced, and replenishing

FIGURE P2.2 A model for the twenty-first century. SOURCE: Created by the authors.

Chapter 8: Strategy: Reimagining Success—Thriving in a Broken World

Chapter 9: Structure: Repairing Failing Institutions—Cementing the Foundations

Chapter 10: Culture: Refreshing Technology—Innovation as a Social Good

The problem is that reworking our thinking, institutions, and shared culture will take significant time. Given the urgency of the crises identified and their sheer scope and scale, time is one thing we do not have. Even as we begin the painstaking process of rebuilding our institutions, economic models, and shared culture, we must dive in with some daring to confront crises that need immediate attention. In so doing, we can begin to move toward a global model of behavior and action that will carry us closer to the outcomes we hope to achieve from our rebuilding efforts. As the world is growing more dynamic, we must learn how to do this perpetually to continually refresh and keep relevant our most important institutions and organizations. We need to use the urgency of our most massive dilemmas to bring the desired future forward faster. What those crises are and how we can undertake the gargantuan task of defeating them are the subject of chapter 11, "Massive and Fast—Problems That Cannot Wait."

To achieve all of this, we need new types of leaders. People who can with some agility rethink our strategies and tactics in practical ways, build more effective and sustainable institutions, alter the dysfunctional dynamics with which we interact and engage each other, and address the world's problems and promote change based on a worldview that is more sustainable and adaptive to our new realities. While juggling this litany of tasks, these leaders will find themselves compelled to steer through political, social, cultural, and strategic pressures and biases that seem quite at odds with each other. I have identified six leadership paradoxes that they will have to reconcile to achieve a better future. That is the subject of chapter 12, "Leadership: Reframing Influence—Balancing Paradoxes."

Although this is a book directed in part at people who lead corporations, large and small governments, institutions, and NGOs, it is also for the rest of us. The problems at our doorsteps are too big and too important for anyone to ignore and decide not to do their part in solving them. Some of what we need to do requires that we change our behavior; some demands new ways of thinking; and some will depend on serious new efforts and greater imagination and creativity.

That actually is the fun part. We have built a world that has had innumerable and unfathomable successes in bringing up the social and economic conditions of many of its residents. Now it will require ingenuity, vision, innovation, energy, focus, new disciplines, and a strong dose of empathy to fix this world so that everybody benefits. Just the thing humans were designed for.

CHAPTER 7

Strategy: Rethinking Economic Growth

Local First

In recent decades—in the heyday of globalization—there was a tidy simplicity to describing the momentum of economic development around the world. A host of countries that had been struggling and were often isolated—mired in poverty with large swaths of their population in need of a first, relatively decent paying job—offered something that companies in the developed world could not resist. Under this arrangement, Japan, Korea, China, and other so-called Asian Tigers held out the prospect of cheap labor and few workplace regulations or environmental rules in exchange for becoming the world's manufacturer or back office. At least in theory, both sides won. The middle class in emerging nations swelled with hundreds of millions more people as GDP growth ballooned. Profits soared and export markets expanded in the dominant economies, where consumers enjoyed low-cost goods and highly skilled workers could take their pick of attractive jobs.

But sometime in the past decade or so, the threads of that orderly formula began to unravel—so much so that now the globalization model no longer works as a reliable framework for economic development for countries already on the development ladder or those still trying to climb onto a lower rung. At the core of this change, the countries that outsourced labor and consumed the products of China, Japan, and Korea are slowly pulling in the reins on that approach as they encourage their companies—often through public and political pressure—to repatriate manufacturing and services to shore up domestic economies.

Simultaneously, multinational companies have begun to lean away from broad international footprints extending deep into low-wage countries, because the surge of populist governments everywhere has added layers of risk and difficulty to creating global supply chains. In addition, labor arbitrage isn't as important as it used to be. The competition is no longer over inexpensive labor in other countries, but increasingly to implement even less costly, smarter, and more capable robots and artificial intelligence tools and programs.

The undermining of globalization has left a vacuum for a new economic development model to emerge. In my view the optimal option for filling this void is a strategy called Local First. That is, self-sustaining, self-contained, continuously improving local economic ecosystems. Perhaps the best argument for choosing a Local First strategy as an improvement on the predominant internationalist framework we've grown accustomed to is the observation that even when globalization appeared to benefit everyone, it didn't. Certainly, the middle class expanded globally along with corporate profits, operational efficiency gains were real, the net prices of most manufactured goods were held in check, and more people participated in the personal technology and communications revolution. But these improvements—primarily captured by GDP growth—only masked the paralyzing negative effects of globalization.

For one thing, individuals who slipped through the jobs market—and there were large blocks of people in every country who could not compete—were invisible; they were the great underemployed and as globalization took hold, they slipped deeper into the shadows. More broadly, GDP figures testified to global prosperity on average, while broad portions of the employed population were experiencing years of income stagnation and decline. GDP results also papered over intangible factors such as environmental degradation, the lack of benefits and the insecurity associated with many jobs, and the diminished quality of life in some communities.

In our 2017 article Colm Kelly and I discussed the chief elements of globalization's dark side—in particular we expressed concern that business gains and social progress were no longer aligned and not even measured or discussed in the same breath anymore.[1] As we noted, this is a relatively new phenomenon. Before globalization became dominant, and even in its earliest stages, business success was intrinsically linked to the success of the community or society within which it operated. Capital was created and primarily remained in the area that its employees and many of its customers came from, even if a portion of it was generated by sales outside the area. Think of the world Adam Smith occupied when he wrote *Wealth of Nations* (1776): if business leaders didn't pay attention to people's needs in their own backyard, they would be lambasted on Sunday in church, they would be ostracized at local town meetings, and they would be shamed into reinvesting their profits into the area, and its people.

In some fashion, everyone from Henry Ford to Andrew Carnegie to Warner von Siemens to Kiichiro Toyoda to Jamsetji Tata began their ultimately vast business empires locally and maintained an intimate connection with their local communities even as their markets grew further and further away. Small- and medium-sized businesses have been even more essential to the economic development in their midst. Indeed, it could be said that without small- and medium-sized companies bolstering jobs expansion and innovation in one circumscribed region after another, countries like Germany, the UK, and the United States would never have enjoyed their leadership position in global markets.

With the rise of multinational corporations, hoisted to the pinnacle by globalization, resources increasingly became concentrated in organizations that didn't have a "home" to which they felt morally obligated to protect and sustain. Their employment base was everywhere and nowhere; their allegiance to their headquarter communities went only as far as the best tax and incentives deals they could wrangle. As Kelly and I observed, their responsibility to deliver a public good and support local development was barely acknowledged.

In fact, many globalization-oriented corporations have not only failed to provide basic tangible benefits for communities they do business in, they also played a troubling role in worsening elements of ADAPT (primarily asymmetry, technological disruption, and lack of trust in institutions). As we wrote, expressing the urgency to establish Local First programs for economic development, "We need to devote more energy to creating thriving communities. Human needs are best identified and managed at a local level. Cities, towns, and villages are the places where social progress and economic success most naturally meet. We need to create conditions for these communities to thrive, with business as a key part of the ecosystem."[2]

Of course, this is not to say that being a global competitor is a losing strategy in all instances. Cities like Barcelona, Moscow, or New York, which uniquely have concentrated educated workforces, excellent universities, deep investment channels, global infrastructure, and governments that support business development, are still in a good position to enjoy gains for the people and cultures of their communities from many facets of globalization. But midtier cities have no chance to beat these larger urban areas at their own game and must begin to be more self-conscious about their economic development strategies, looking inward more than they have for many decades. In fact, when giant cities use their existing competitiveness to absorb global resources, they often ruin smaller cities in their countries by pulling more attention, investment, and human capital away from those places.

To provide a blueprint for what a locally focused economic development program might look like—although significant social and cultural distinctions will, virtually by definition, separate one local program from another—a set of projects in Armenia is a suitable place to start.

A Local First Model

Ruben Vardanyan is an Armenian-born philanthropist, entrepreneur, and investment banker who, along with cosponsors Veronika Zonabend,

Noubar Afeyan, Pierre Gurdjian, and Arman Jilavian, has initiated a number of locally oriented projects across Armenia designed to, as Vardanyan puts it, "create great places, develop thriving people and promote uplifting values, hence our work in social and economic development, education and leadership, and humanitarian values." Perhaps the most apt distillation of Vardanyan's work is captured in Figure 7.1, which my team and I put together with Vardanyan's philanthropic organization IDeA (Initiatives for Development of Armenia).

This model is best suited for locations with an identifiable, collective past—core traditions that can be embraced and modernized to foster an environment for change and growth. Each element in the figure contains a set of components that should be addressed simultaneously and work together to form a system of local development. The left side of the figure targets the physical, institutional, and economic infrastructure of a place. It calls for holistic education to prepare talent for the future; a self-renewing economic ecosystem that stimulates job creation through entrepreneurial activity; and programs to promote well-being in its broadest sense, including healthcare, recreational activity, the environment, a sense of justice, transparency, and fairness (the factors that make people want to claim a place as home).

The right side of the figure focuses on the development of a positive cultural narrative, building on a shared sense of identity and capturing the mind, soul, and heart of the locale. It is about celebrating the area's unique qualities and successes but also does not shy away from the negative narrative that likely exists in a place that is not thriving. There is a need to transform the grief of a place's history or economic and social dynamics into hope and positive renewal. The two sides are joined by the bridge in the center—a bridge made up of people, the broad talent base required to implement both sides. These are people with rare capabilities to understand how systems function and are interconnected, who can promote and catalyze change within and across these systems. These people must have the imagination to envision the possibilities for the area, despite existing constraints.

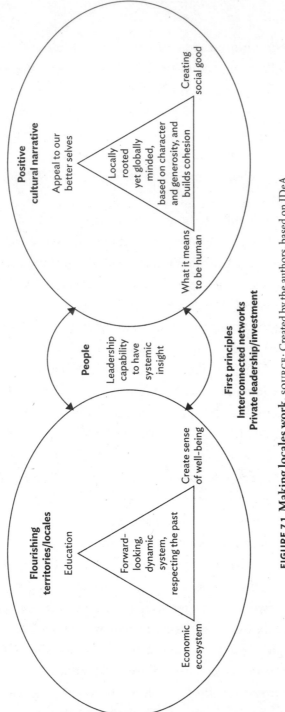

FIGURE 7.1 Making locales work. SOURCE: Created by the authors, based on IDeA (Initiatives for Development of Armenia).

To illustrate how this works, let's look at a team project that IDeA calls the Tatev Revival.[3] At the heart of this project is the restoration of the Tatev Monastery, a medieval center of religion, culture, and learning in southern Armenia. This has been a monumental effort because most of the buildings on the Tatev grounds were in serious disrepair, neglected for centuries. During the reconstruction the central social role of the monastery has been reemphasized as one that knits together the local community under the banner of university-level education that attracts students interested in humanities, religious study, or the sciences.

This has elevated the Tatev region community in numerous ways. Social scientists and other researchers have moved into the area to study feudal conditions and mores; the Tatev Monastery Children's Choir, composed of dozens of local children, is gaining in renown via its performances throughout Armenia; local schools are being rebuilt; and the first environmental preservation projects in the area are underway. Before this project, Tatev was a forgotten region, slipping further and further away from modernity and prosperity and largely unknown to tourists. Today, it is an open, outward-looking, and economically well-positioned area, connected to the greater world around it through a tramway, part of the Tatev Revival, which transformed the journey to the monastery from a one-hour ride along zigzagging roads into a twelve-minute extraordinary excursion that travels high over the mountains and gorges of the Tatev region. These elements of the project exemplify the right-hand portion of Figure 7.1—the positive cultural narrative.

The left side of the figure is evidenced by the advancement of educational opportunities in the area and the monastery itself as well as the evolving economic ecosystem growing up around the Tatev project. High-quality jobs were created to manage and run the tramway, and more than twenty bed-and-breakfasts and Airbnbs as well as restaurants and cafes have opened. Beyond that, entrepreneurs have flocked into the area to receive business and legal advice from IDeA and set up a range of small service operations—many involving well-being activities such as healthcare and recreational pursuits—for the local community and tourists. The large numbers of people involved in this spurt of economic opportunities as well as the leadership that IDeA is bringing to this project populate the center of the figure.

One essential facet of the Tatev campaign that should not be overlooked—primarily because it is critical to the Local First model—is that the most effective first step is often to find a centerpiece project out of which a much larger ecosystem of economic development and community coherence can emerge. In the context of Tatev that centerpiece was the tramway, appropriately called the Wings of Tatev, which served as the conduit to "fly" people and modernity into the region that had been lost to time, forging a climate in which growth and change built upon the traditions of the past can thrive.

As we examined the way Vardanyan's approach to the Local First model works in practice, we pinpointed four principles that are essential to success:

1. Building a local economy is not for the impatient—it takes focus, preparation, and time—and is not an inexpensive proposition. Vardanyan and his team view their projects through twenty-year time horizons.

2. Outside investors in Local First projects must show by example that they care about the community they are investing in.

3. Any Local First effort must begin with a real understanding of what makes the locale unique and what the underlying positive or negative narrative is that will serve as the foundation for the project. Innovation not placed atop a locale's history, social customs, and culture will not be sustainable. Negative narratives, such as the Armenian genocide (which IDeA is taking up through its Aurora Humanitarian Initiative), should not be ignored; if they are, they could become a whispered source of failure that continues to burden rather than elevate and cohere a community.[4]

4. Local First ideas should be pioneering, borrowing from the past but addressing the needs of a community today and into the future.

My Adopted Home: Durham, North Carolina

Although it isn't often viewed this way, Local First projects have saved communities in developed countries as well—some call it gentrification, others urban renewal—and they have been responsible for phoenix-like revivals that are in many ways remarkable. Take, for example, Durham, North Carolina. When my wife and I arrived in Durham as newly minted professors some thirty-eight years ago, the city of 162,000 residents had one real hotel, one bar, a hollowed-out downtown, and boarded-up tobacco warehouses ringed by razor wire. It also had a gerrymandered educational system that sent the children of wealthy (mostly white) parents to decent county schools, while poorer kids went to barely functioning city facilities. Durham once had a thriving black commercial and cultural area, home to the largest collection of African American businesses per capita in the United States, but when we arrived, it had been paved over to make room for a highway. I remember talking with a city renewal expert who believed Durham would never be a city in which people would want to live again.

An unlikely combination of three people came together to prove him wrong: Jim Goodmon, one of North Carolina's richest businesspersons and the head of Capital Broadcasting Company, who is a prominent and respected owner of area TV stations as well as the Durham Bulls, a Triple-A minor league team made famous in the film *Bull Durham*; Bill Bell, Durham's second African American mayor and the city's longest serving top official, elected in 2001; and Tallman Trask, executive vice president of Duke University, who, among other things, had responsibility for the university's real estate activities. Prior to their teaming up on the construction project that would run through the first decade of the 2000s and would remake Durham's trajectory, there had been lots of investment in the city, but most of it was to the west of downtown near Duke University or in the very south of the city near the burgeoning Research Triangle Park. The problem was that Durham's urban core would never revitalize if the investments continued to be isolated in the more upscale areas to the west or south of the city.

What Goodmon, Bell, and Trask saw that no others did before them was the potential of the dilapidated area just on the southern edge of downtown that had been the original home of the Duke family tobacco business. This fifteen-acre campus with more than a dozen buildings had been shuttered some years earlier as Duke's venerable American Tobacco Company fell into decline before being acquired by Brown and Williamson. The ten-foot razor wire fence surrounding the facility dissuaded everyone but the drug dealers from entering the site. Next to the campus was vacant land, an automotive dealership, Durham's single original hotel—now on its last legs—and more empty warehouses. Goodmon, Bell, and Trask felt that if they could turn this area around, it would be possible to connect it to the development in the west and bring downtown back to life.

The men linked their renewal program to two vital elements in the history of Durham, both of which had been seen as evidence that the city was declining: the tobacco plants and the Durham Bulls. Similar to the Wings of Tatev, these centerpiece projects would serve as the springboard for Durham's renaissance. Around 2000, Goodmon risked his own money to purchase the American Tobacco campus as the start of an effort to remodel the site into a multiuse facility comprising office space, research centers, restaurants, places to walk or sit over long conversations, and entertainment. Trask reduced Goodmon's financial exposure by preleasing significant space at the site for Duke administration to relocate and strongly encouraging other employers around the county to do the same. Bell ensured that the city government backed this effort by publicly speaking up for its completion, minimizing the red tape, and ginning up resident support. Goodmon's decision to undertake the transformation of the tobacco plants came on the heels of Capitol City's purchase of land adjacent to the American Tobacco site a few years earlier, where a new modern Bulls stadium was erected to replace a ramshackle, barely useable structure north of the city.

These construction projects changed Durham. Suddenly the downtown area seemed like a desirable investment again. The two miles or so between Duke's campus and this new vibrant area attracted additional restaurateurs, entrepreneurs drawn in by the relatively inexpensive space in a cool area near the university campus, new developers, and young professionals wanting to live and raise their children in an area with funky character and so much to offer. Many of the early business and restaurant owners in the area were immigrants, giving Durham a more diverse and inclusive aspect than it had ever had. To accommodate the changing landscape, the County Commissioners and the city's educational boards are working to integrate the two school systems. The once derided tobacco factories and the Durham Bulls are both celebrated with pride by city residents again. Of course, there is a lot more to do, but Durham is now a thriving, diverse city that people want to live in—a place to build lives, families, and careers. It's a far cry from the city our children's friends refused to visit because it was too frightening and there was nothing to see there anyway.

Local Entrepreneurs: The Building Blocks

This chapter has explored two very large Local First projects with lots of resources behind them, but Local First economic development need not be so imposing. Indeed, it can begin in less grandiose efforts—yet in many ways achieve an equally consequential outcome. I came across two remarkable Local First efforts that fit this de minimis category at an event called Slush in December 2018. Slush is the world's leading start-up and tech conference. One of its highlights is a competition in which entrepreneurs developing businesses that serve social needs are invited to pitch their ideas to the attendees. I was a judge in 2018, when I met the two memorable winners, both from Zambia, with Local First projects: Muzalema Mwanza's Safe Motherhood Alliance and Mwila Kangwa's Agripredict.

Mwanza says she "came face to face with some of the challenges pregnant women face in rural areas" when she herself became pregnant. For
one thing, it was too expensive for most mothers in rural Zambia to go
to clinics; instead, they had self-managed births at home, often in squalid
conditions. For another, when diagnostic tools were available, they were
primitive and most of the time there was no one assisting in the births
who actually understood how to operate the tools or how the birthing process should work. An engineer by training but now a social entrepreneur,
Mwanza came up with a straightforward solution: a sanitary kit containing
all the materials necessary to support the birthing process and a program
to train local women to use this equipment for facilitating clean and successful home births. To maintain quality control and keep costs down, she
sourced and manufactured these kits locally. As a result, she was able to
price her first products at only 25 Euros.

Mwanza has expanded the Safe Motherhood Alliance to design a series
of low-cost diagnostic tools that support maternal and newborn health,
which can be used at mobile clinics and small hospitals with technologies
like Doppler ultrasound readings via smartphone. She sees her efforts
through the Safe Motherhood Alliance as a way to build economic development through the encouragement of a grassroots healthcare sector in even
the smallest communities. Her ultimate goal is to scale the business so that
it extends to nearly every rural village in Zambia, linking them to each other
to share innovation and expertise, and over time introducing her work into
the rest of Africa and beyond to other regions with similar challenges.

The other Zambian entrepreneur was Mwila Kangwa, the founder of
Agripredict. A soft-spoken engineer, Kangwa focused directly on how the
economic system lets down tens of thousands of Zambia's farmers, many
of whom live a subsistence existence from one growing season to the next.
Rather than employing an economic model that attempts to ensure that
farmers survive year to year if a crop fails, the Zambian government has
mostly ignored the plight of the growers. As a result, a diseased crop can
be disastrous, resulting in family starvation or loss of land. Most Zambian

farmers have no tools or wherewithal to diagnose a failing crop or mitigate the problem before it becomes untreatable.

Kangwa's solution is a smartphone-based program that allows a farmer to send to Agripredict a picture of the diseased plant and receive back a disease diagnosis, options for treatment, and the location of a dealer that has the necessary supplies to mitigate the problem. Agripredict has caught on; after only a year more than twenty-two thousand Zambian farmers have signed up for the service. Kangwa plans to use the success of this product to develop other programs that can help local farmers develop more efficient growing methods, expand their crop types, add value to their harvested crops, and, as a result, raise their economic strata well above a subsistence level. The effects of pest infestations and droughts on agricultural development have affected national and regional food security. Small-scale farmers do not have the tools to mitigate or prevent these diseases and predict weather conditions (most rely on natural seasonal conditions). Furthermore, the current method for information dissemination is costly, extremely slow, and at times ineffective. The control of agricultural pests is critical to sustainable agricultural development.

◎   ◎   ◎

These Local First efforts are emblematic of the work of thousands of entrepreneurs across the globe who are trying to devise local solutions for local problems and in turn develop dynamic local economies. Stitched together, these campaigns exemplify a model that in nearly every important way differs from the far-flung industrial global supply chains of the late twentieth century. Of course, industrial multinationalism is not dead, but it is no longer the answer for economic development in many local regions. Indeed, most of the villages, towns, and cities that have yet to enjoy economic advantages or are being left behind will need to find ways to create a dynamic and thriving economic, educational, and cultural system with a compelling local storyline to provide opportunities for the billions of people that they are responsible for.

Having watched the emergence of Local First ideas, I have some optimism that human ingenuity in these less advantaged places throughout the world will capably unearth innovative answers to address this challenge. Moreover, it will happen more quickly if these local entrepreneurs can count on resources in the form of organizational, operational, and design expertise as well as financial support from the private sector and philanthropists in developed economies. Perhaps to our disappointment we have learned grudgingly that the axiom "a rising tide lifts all boats" is not quite the self-evident truth we once thought it was. Instead, today it may be more appropriate to view the embryonic flow of a local rivulet as the most reliable precursor of an economic waterfall for a local developing region.

CHAPTER 8

Strategy:
Reimagining Success

Thriving in a Broken World

Chapter 7 covered the value of local initiatives in addressing our urgent crises and presented them as a potentially more effective approach than global, national, or even multinational campaigns. That is chiefly because we believe that to deal quickly and effectively with the dilemmas confronting us, grassroots, entrepreneurial, public–private, targeted, and small- or medium-sized group innovation is essential and probably represents the majority of solutions. Out of singular breakthroughs—discrete campaigns that, for instance, reduce asymmetry by seeding economic opportunities in a small region; establish new institutions that directly attend the needs of the local populace and further the goals of the campaign; and implement technology that improves people's lives—ecosystems and partnerships can emerge to replicate these successes in other places, scaling resources, knowledge, and ideas.

However, none of this is to deny the important responsibility of nations to help alter the disturbing path that we find ourselves on. Indeed, broad, national policies are essential to mitigate some of the most endemic and deep-seated aspects of the crises. These policies include tax regulations that more fairly balance contributions from the wealthy and the less well-off, or immigration rules that effectively navigate diverse views about outsiders within the country, or safeguards to protect people's privacy from technological intrusion, or employment programs aimed at preparing the next generation of workers to take advantage of opportunities that artificial intelligence offers, rather than being defeated by it, or climate policy essential to diminishing the production of heat-gathering gases.

Only national governments have the reach and the wherewithal to deliver broad policy agendas for improving the lives of their citizens, which can then serve as springboards and support systems for local and entrepreneurial programs. Indeed, if nothing else, central governments should consider big policy initiatives to ensure their own survival: in nearly every country distrust of the ruling class is so elevated that national administrations cannot afford to delay proving that they can provide a political and social environment in which a better future for people within their borders can blossom.

Unfortunately, despite the important position that governing bodies could hold, most of the discussions at the national level around the world demonstrate that few are prepared for or capable of tackling the crises identified in this book. Attempts at finding solutions primarily lack will or imagination and are reflective of a fractured world, predicated upon outmoded notions from the last century—many of which ultimately were responsible for today's global problems—and preoccupied with satisfying the gluttony of polarization instead of seeking a shared future. This is not an avenue to success; quite to the contrary, to navigate today's difficult global landscape, every nation needs an explicit strategy for addressing the crises arising from ADAPT in a manner that creates a positive and all-embracing environment. Rather than view their achievements solely through a narrow metric—most prominently GDP, which is blind to the distinct economic and social conditions that individuals in a country live under—nations should also measure themselves by the quality of life and the social goods their residents enjoy and by how inclusive their society is, or, put another way, by how few people are left behind.

This strategy—focused on what we call interdependent, inclusive success—is generally absent from the international scene today. But it is available to all countries, including those that seem the least likely to adopt such an approach. Perhaps the best and most surprising example is the UK, which despite Brexit is in an extraordinary position to become an enabler of global interdependence in a fractured world in ways that buoy the prospects of all of its citizens at home. In fact, Brexit has left the UK with few strategic choices but to be such an enabler.

The UK has an opportunity to make a meaningful impact precisely because it is not among the four rule writers or geopolitical chieftains vying for spheres of influence that we wrote about in chapter 2   China, the European Union, Russia, and the United States. The world is fracturing at an accelerated pace and tensions and uncertainty surrounding the rule writers have veered off in so many unanticipated directions that many businesses have pressed the pause button before committing to future activities in these countries. For instance, PwC's 2019 survey of global CEOs found that only 27 percent of respondents viewed the United States as a good investment alternative, down from 46 percent the year before; China fell to 24 percent from 33 percent.[1]

To get a sense of the intrinsic features of a global enabler, and why the UK could be suited for that task, it is useful to look at postwar twentieth-century Singapore, which exemplified the vital role global enablers can play as well as the outsized success they can have at home. Sputtering and poor at the time of its separation from Britain and then Malaysia in the mid-1960s, Singapore was transformed under the leadership of Lee Kuan Yew into a hub for multinational companies (MNCs). Implementing policies that put the tiny island nation on a firm financial footing, including preventing the internationalization of the Singapore dollar, limiting the operations of foreign banks, and rooting out corruption in interactions between the public and private sector, Lee enticed some of the world's largest companies to set up operations in Singapore. In the process, foreign investment exploded and global trade in and out of its ports ballooned.

While providing a haven for trade and multinational operations—serving as the grease for globalization, a place for MNCs to safely and profitably do business outside of their home markets—Lee and his government also focused inward on Singaporeans. As Singapore's cashflow exploded, Lee's administration sponsored rules requiring local banks to support industrial development and infrastructure projects that would provide jobs and jumpstart the local economy. Unemployment dropped from about 15 percent in 1960 to 2 percent now, a period in which per capita GDP rose nearly sixty times. Because of liberal immigration policies, Singapore's population more than tripled in that time, providing a growing labor pool for manufacturing and technology-based businesses. In addition, tens of thousands of skilled workers are produced by Singapore's top-ranked educational system, another outgrowth of Lee's interior spending priorities.

Lee resigned as Singapore's prime minister in 1990 (after thirty-one years) but stayed on in various advisory roles until his death in 2015. As much as his forward-looking policies altered Singapore's less-than-stellar narrative arc, Lee's leadership style was also indispensable. He embraced an approach that we call *strategic executor* (see chapter 12 for a deeper discussion on this and other leadership paradoxes). These are people who can articulate a strategy, understand the ways it may need to evolve to generate consistently positive results, and execute this strategy with both immediate needs and longer-term potentially shifting conditions in mind. This leadership tension is rooted in setting goals and continually measuring how closely they are met, while not being afraid or too proud to change direction if the metrics are wanting. Interviewed about his leadership tenets, Lee said: "Presented with a difficulty or major problem or an assessment of conflicting facts, I review what alternatives I have if my proposed solution doesn't work. I choose a solution which offers a higher probability of success, but if it fails, I have some other way. Never a dead end."[2]

Singapore's success story aligned perfectly with a period of expanding globalization and internationalization of financial and economic networks; other places in the world thrived during that time in similar ways (for example, Dubai and Ireland). Although the global environment has changed quite a bit and the desired outcomes are different today, four characteristics that contributed most to Singapore's emergence on the world stage are noteworthy (and still relevant): (1) an advantageous geographic position; (2) an excellent educational system—in particular, elite universities are crucial; (3) a strong rule of law, which translates into being a stable, pluralistic democracy and a safe place to do business; and (4) perhaps often overlooked, an inclusive society that welcomes outsiders and is guided by policies that are meant to improve the well-being and social status of all strata in every community. Inclusive countries command respect and trust around the world and are consequently perceived as attractive places to study, live, and navigate differences.

The modern successors to Singapore will need these and one other important attribute: considering the urgency to address intractable global dilemmas and the power wielded by the four rule writers, today's enablers will have to be of a size that will make them already significant in the global economy, not so large as to be threatening but large enough to have a big impact.

The UK's Opportunity

Although the decision to leave the European Union casts a shadow over any discussions about the UK these days, had the Brexit referendum never been held, many of the underlying economic and social challenges that the UK will face post-Brexit would still threaten the nation's future. But they might have been papered over and neglected, as they have for many years. Indeed, Brexit represents such a potentially revolutionary shift in the UK's prospects that by compelling its leaders and citizens to address the shortcomings of their country or chance drifting into irrelevance, Brexit may redound to the country's benefit.

Among the most pressing issues bedeviling the UK is the wealth disparity between individuals (the top 10 percent of households control almost half of all Britain's total wealth), between London and rural regions, and across generations. The UK's manufacturing sector has shrunk faster than any other Western country—from about 17 percent of GDP in 1990 to 9 percent now. The UK's technological innovation barely registers today, except in a few targeted areas such as materials science. The population is aging quickly, putting those three groups discussed in chapter 2 at risk: those about to retire with very little capital preserved and no, or limited, pension; those who are midcareer, have taken on sizable financial obligations, and are now threatened by technological disruption and economic loss even more so than before because of Brexit; and university students graduating without the right education and with overwhelming debt.

Yet even with these core problems, which are not dissimilar to challenges other developed Western countries are facing, the UK is well situated to be a central force in the world—an enabler to an inclusive rebirth of the global order that serves everyone, not only the most fortunate—and simultaneously improve the fraught conditions that many of its citizens endure. Viewing the UK through a different lens—one that focuses on how well Britain's assets stack up against the characteristics needed by countries that would play an enabler role—a different picture emerges.

> *Geographic position.* The UK sits between two of the great powers—the European Union (EU) and the United States—which are experiencing increasing tension on a number of fronts, making the UK a natural choice for broker, buffer, and convener.

> *Education.* The UK's university system is the envy of the world; five colleges are consistently ranked in the global top twenty-five and several others are in the running. Top UK schools have been synonymous with scholarly endeavor and academic achievement, not for decades but for centuries. This matters because the United States— the country that has traditionally benefited the most from attracting the best and brightest students from around the world—is increasingly less than welcoming to people who wish to emigrate for academic reasons.

> *Rule of law.* In spite of Brexit, the UK is seen as a relatively stable place, known for a strong justice system, a deep sense of morality and care

in decision making—overall, a stable pluralistic democratic system. Because of this, London stands atop the world as a major center for finance and professional services. Post-Brexit, a more independent position might enhance London and the UK's profile in this regard.

> *Inclusiveness.* In the UK, diversity is generally respected. Many people consider London their second home and view it as both comfortable and relatively safe. It continues to be a highly desirable destination for those seeking to emigrate in search of a better life.

On this point, last year I visited the London School of Economics (LSE). The entrance to the campus is a corridor that gives the sensation of walking through a narrow alley and, as a consequence, you cannot help but bump into a few people along the way. In fact, I literally bumped into a group of students (who I learned were from Bangladesh, Chile, China, Ethiopia, Saudi Arabia, and the United States) engaged in an energetic debate about what new forms global governance should take. Naturally, I joined the discussion, if for no other reason than it was a fascinating intellectual excursion through the issues covered in this book.

I asked the students why they were at LSE. To a person, their answer was, "Where else could you have this conversation?" What they implied in that question may not quite be true—I can think of campuses in the United States, other parts of Europe, and even India where these discussions could also occur—but their enthusiasm about LSE and the city was telling. After all, while these conversations may not be limited to London, the self-conscious sentiment that it is the only city where you will find them shows how attractive the UK is to the world's brightest young people.

> *Economic size.* Although a relatively small nation, the UK has the fifth largest GDP in the world.

The UK's advantages are a ray of hope in the midst of the country's upheaval. If it chose to be an enabler—and use its opportunity to create a better nation post-Brexit both as a world citizen and as a home for all of its own people—a coordinated effort across six strategic areas would be required. These six areas are already in part touched by various UK policies, but they need to be shaped into a coherent and intentional whole. Below are our suggestions:

1. *Target the world's top talent to study and, in some cases, build businesses in the UK.* To import the brightest people from around the world, the UK should actively promote itself as the place that welcomes the most intelligent students and support this initiative with path-to-citizenship and competition-based immigration policies that open the door wide for these students and allow the most capable to remain and build businesses after their education is over. To avoid additional tax burden on UK citizens for educating immigrants, these students should be charged the full tuition and ancillary fees, while privately funded scholarships could support top-of-the-pyramid students who cannot afford university costs. In considering this strategy, it is worth remembering that many Silicon Valley start-ups were built and are now staffed in large part by immigrants who initially came to the United States as students. In fact, the founders of twenty-one of America's 91 billion-dollar start-up companies initially arrived in the United States as international students.[3]

2. *Attract domestic and foreign capital to invest in innovation centers adjacent to UK universities.* To build its own Silicon Valleys, the UK should actively support the connection between universities and nascent innovation hubs through grants and tax incentives, but also tout the advantages the country has to make the broader case to CEOs and investors that the UK is an advantageous place to invest in. To address regional economic disparities, a focus on developing these innovation hubs in locations outside of London (and not just Oxford and Cambridge) is essential. This strategy should target the decline in manufacturing by supporting Factory 4.0 industrial advances. Products made in the UK out of this program should have natural connections to the overseas home markets

from which the founders of some of these innovation-based companies came as students.

3. *Focus research and education around a few critical areas.* The Silicon Valley ecosystem approach is founded on the idea that the educational curriculum (for instance, at Palo Alto's Stanford University) is aligned with the industrial strategy that has evolved in the region's innovation hub. In like manner, the UK should direct its research funding to certain topics of activity on which the country wants to build its global reputation. This is particularly important in the post-Brexit world, when EU funding will be eliminated. Ideally, the research areas would address major integrated problems that humanity faces today. They should include ADAPT-related issues like new global order in the area of deglobalization, materials science, medicine and healthcare, improving quality of life for the elderly, alternative energy, and soft capitalism (in which employees and customers share in a company's success rather than just fuel it).

4. *Place special emphasis on developing technology-savvy humanists.* We purposely omitted one research area from the problems that the UK should focus on primarily because it is so overarching that it needs to be viewed as a separate, undiluted priority—to wit, humanizing technology or ensuring that technology such as artificial intelligence, robotics, social media, communications devices, and global networks serve people's most pressing needs without threatening their well-being. To do this, the UK should formulate an explicit curricular strategy focused on developing talent in the most critical domains of technology, which also ensures that the students are taught to appreciate the unique characteristics of human systems and indeed of humanity itself. Done right, this strategy would enable UK universities to better prepare the country's brightest students to navigate a future with technology playing an increasingly central role. As part of lifelong learning programs, this approach would develop an entrepreneurial class and professional talent

able to build and design useful technology while mitigating its potential negative side effects—in other words, a technology that is inclusive in its benefits.

5. *Negotiate free trade agreements with the critical players.* Without the EU as an open trading partner, the UK has no choice but to develop relatively unencumbered trade agreements with major global players and increasingly influential regions—the United States, China, India, the Middle East, and critical parts of Africa. These trade discussions in emerging regions and countries should be viewed as an opportunity to craft explicit agreements intended to develop talent in, for instance, India, the Middle East, and Africa. These arrangements should be aimed at accelerating the growth of universities and educational competency in UK trading partners through cooperative programs with UK schools. This will create natural venues in which to market ideas, services, or products manufactured in the UK and serve as a vehicle for identifying and attracting the best talent to tap for future entrepreneurial and innovative ventures.

6. *Make the UK a central node in a multinodal world.* The UK should take advantage of its somewhat unique geopolitical position—that is, its proximity and long-standing relationship with the rest of Europe and its independence from it as well as its friendly relations with the United States—to establish itself as a relatively neutral place that world leaders and global thinktanks can meet to discuss and debate prevailing issues and seek agreement. By playing this role, the UK would further cement itself as a reliable and trustworthy financial and commercial center even during turbulent times.

Taken as a group, this "enabler" strategy points to a plethora of positive outcomes for the UK. Viewed from inside the country, this strategy sets up new educational standards and goals that will improve the preparation of graduates for the types of jobs that will be most valuable as the future unfolds. In addition, it helps determine what those jobs will be as it reduces the UK's competitiveness gap in technology, reinvigorates the industrial and service economy base, and develops pathways for innovative companies to emerge out of new ideas. Through programs aimed at lifelong learning, it retools midcareer professionals displaced by automation for better jobs and overall raises professionalism and compensation of basic service workers and tradespeople. There are gains for retirees as well. This approach should create a significantly larger tax base from which to draw support for necessary public services. If an explicit focus for research is put on medicine and health, less expensive solutions for sustained healthcare should result.

There would also be consequential benefits to the rest of the world. With the decline of many postwar institutions and the shredding of old alliances, the world desperately needs a place to convene, leaving their weapons at the door, so to speak. Although a primary focus of this strategy is to bring a greater infusion of talent to the UK, some meaningful percentage of that talent will eventually return dividends to home countries—and perhaps encourage a spirit of shared mission and community. Perhaps most intriguingly, the UK would be crafting a new narrative for itself, badly needed in times when the country's residents increasing feel like they are living in a country adrift without a shared story to bind it and thus have lost control over their own fate.

The Curious Tale of Dofasco

This chapter began by examining the weight of nations in a world that is fractured and that will increasingly have to turn to individuals and local initiatives for solutions to and activism against seemingly insoluble crises. But while looking at big global plans that nations can implement, it would be a mistake to not consider how this reflects on what corporations should and could do in a similarly large and inclusive fashion that protects and advances the well-being of all of their employees, the communities in which they operate, and the world. After all, each company has a huge influence on the quality of life of anywhere from a handful to hundreds of thousands of workers, from blue collar to executive, around the corner and around the world. They impact equally the communities that surround their factories, warehouses, and office spaces. How seriously companies approach their obligations to their workers, customers, partners, and environs—in similar manner to the way that nations advance their responsibilities to their citizens and their global partners—could determine their own short-term success and long-term relevance in the world.

Just as GDP is a poor metric for gauging the overall satisfaction, economic optimism, and prospects for the future of a nation's residents and communities, shareholder value is an overly relied upon yardstick that is equally inadequate when measuring a corporation's performance. Certainly, it is an apt benchmark for determining what shareholders get from their investments, but it is woefully agnostic about the equity of employee participation in the company as well as the impact of the organization on the surrounding communities, customers, suppliers, and the broader environment that it comes in contact with. In other words, shareholder value is indifferent to the elements of interdependence and inclusiveness that we believe are essential to a company's success and to overcoming the worst ramifications of the crises. As with nations, few corporations today appear to be viewing their role through a sufficiently wide-angled lens.

In my memory, a company that convincingly demonstrated the significance and efficacy of a more interdependent and inclusive approach the last time the world faced a period of existential threats was Dofasco Steel, which I got to know well firsthand. Earlier in this book I shared that I was fortunate to have been born and raised in Hamilton, Ontario, when it was a thriving prosperous city. I was lucky that my father worked for Dofasco, at the time the second largest employer and contributor to the tax base in Hamilton. Dofasco was founded in 1912 by Canadian industrialist Clifton Sherman, who named the firm Dominion Foundries and Steel Company, later shortened to Dofasco. Spurred by the shift from iron to steel in railway construction, the company was tremendously profitable until the Great

Depression in 1929, when the global market for manufactured products collapsed. Clifton, with his brother Frank, who had joined the business soon after it debuted, responded to the Depression with a set of actions that were unimaginable at the time—and to a large degree now as well.

Instead of pulling in the reins of the business and alienating its workers with steps that would harm its employees and essentially blame them for the downturn, Dofasco's management instituted policies that treated the company as a single community and everyone working there from top to bottom as equal. They had a sense that this method of managing the business would pay off when economic conditions stabilized—and indeed these policies became core principles and emblemized the corporate culture in ways that would guide the firm for decades to come. Rather than laying off hundreds of workers, Dofasco reduced the workweek for everyone in the firm while trimming compensation for the most senior people and then using those savings to support the families of employees who couldn't survive on a short week's salary. On top of that, having seeded the notion that all Dofasco workers were fighting the same struggle together, the Shermans set up a suggestion process in which any employee's idea for how to improve operations or customer service was taken seriously. And they put into place Canada's first profit-sharing plan.

Over time other elements grew to support this inclusive culture, including the one I remember most fondly: the annual holiday party, which was held at one of the mills that was decked out for the festive season. In some years, nearly fifty thousand employees and their families would attend the party; every family was given a food package and every child left with a gift. Well before it was a common thing to do, Dofasco also set up programs to support jobs training, arts and cultural projects, and environmental protection in Hamilton as well as in the towns built around the iron ore mines the company owned in northern Canada.

This management approach was an extraordinary success. When the Depression lifted, particularly as the World War II industrial expansion took hold, Dofasco was in a privileged position with a sufficiently large, well-trained, and motivated workforce to meet the ballooning demand for steel. Its competitors were playing catch-up while Dofasco generated record profits, a track record that would continue through the 1980s. By then the third generation of the family had taken control and management had slipped out of the hands of the Shermans and into the technocratic arms of outside MBA-trained leaders who, through their education, gained a fondness for the importance of shareholder value. The company's culture lost its progressive aura and in 1990, during a global recession, Dofasco was acquired in a hostile takeover by Luxembourg-based Arcelor, the world's second largest steel producer, which itself was purchased by the No. 1 steel company (India's Mittal) three months later. Today, Dofasco is a much smaller company that slips in and out of profitability—and no longer a beacon of enlightened and inclusive corporate management in Hamilton.

Some may consider Dofasco a quaint piece of the past, but actually the company's history is extremely relevant today. Of course, there are obvious differences: many companies have a much broader footprint than Dofasco ever had and consequently the effect that organizations can have on their workers, partners, and the larger societies in which they operate is much greater. This in turn means that the harm that can result from an overly narrow view of success as well as the potential benefits of having a more interdependent, inclusive perception of success are significantly elevated. What is still remarkably applicable today from the Dofasco story is that shareholder gains need not be at odds with an inclusive "do more good than bad" strategy. In other words, particularly in times of crisis, interdependence and inclusiveness are perhaps the most valuable strategic markers.

◎ ◎ ◎

This chapter illustrated how countries with the right characteristics could simultaneously reposition themselves to better navigate the world we now live in and improve the lives of their own citizens and the rest of the globe. We provided a window into how corporations should consider this strategy because their success too depends on operating strategies that benefit not just shareholders but all critical constituents.

Although we focused on the UK, a similar effort should be undertaken by every country: consider the challenges specific to that country, identify its strengths and weaknesses in being able to address those challenges, and develop a clear strategy for positioning itself for inclusive success for all of its citizens by effectively navigating its global interdependence. Although there is a clear need to motivate activism and devise solutions for global crises in entities and institutions both below and above the country level, nations are still the most meaningful political units in the world today.

CHAPTER 9

Structure:
Repairing Failing Institutions

Cementing the Foundations

The term *institution* covers a lot of territory. Political, health, legal, and financial systems are institutions. So are tax codes and the media. Of course, schools, the police, charities, and religions are as well. A diverse group, to be sure. But one thing institutions all have in common is that they play a decisive role in the smooth running of our societies—local and global. When our institutions are working right, they provide stability.[1] We expect certain things from them—a fair trial, the same university degree requirements for all of us, and balanced news reporting, for example. And unless they are corrupted, they generally live up to our expectations. By default, institutions change slowly, and their constancy has engendered widespread trust in them.

But these are not normal times and institutions don't have the luxury now to play by their normal rules. In eras of relentless disruption and global political and social fracturing—and deep-seated fears that the speed of change could upend the world order permanently to the advantage of a few and the disadvantage of many—institutions must adapt. Going a little further, they must learn how to disrupt themselves to keep pace with threatening economic, political, and social trends. In so doing, modernized institutions would perform again their traditional role of preserving the fabric that we need to hold us together and make progress into a difficult future. Unfortunately, many of our institutions are already failing at this and thus are targets of enmity and increasingly seen as irrelevant.

There is a host of substantial, well-researched, and verified analyses on managing change in large organizations, but the purpose of this chapter is not to take such a broad view.[2] Instead, through the stories of four extraordinary individuals who have boldly reconceived the operating fundamentals of their waning institutions, we provide a four-step roadmap for institutions to maintain their vital place in our lives in a period that is not easily suited for them. The first three individuals profiled in this chapter tackled failure at institutions we identified in chapter 4 as exemplars of how widespread and damaging institutional dysfunction has become—namely, media, global multilateral organizations, and education. The fourth individual profiled offers insight into how institutions can and must reconnect with the local communities they are intended to serve. Without that, institutional failure is preordained. Although the challenges institutions face are enormous, these stories demonstrate that great leaders who adopt strategies targeted at protecting their institutions from failure can rekindle their institutions to play the essential role of stabilizing and improving society while amplifying the social and economic progress that they were designed for.

Step 1. Media:
Identify the Core Principles, Then Revitalize Them

The institution known as the fourth estate has fallen on hard times. Under pressure from technology and polarization, it is failing noticeably in its essential role as the gatekeeper of the news that matters and the distributor of unbiased facts to a world that is drowning in information and becoming less able to separate truth from fiction. However, one media organization, Pearson Plc (whose properties included Penguin Books, the *Economist*, and *The Financial Times*) was able to buck this trend and avoid succumbing to the forces stacked up against it.

Credit for propping up Pearson during its most challenging period primarily goes to Marjorie Scardino, who had an untraditional journey to eventually become the CEO of one of the UK's most iconic (and wobbling) institutions. Born in Arizona and raised in Texarkana, Scardino was a rodeo barrel racer early in life, stayed in Texas through college and her graduation from Baylor University, completed law school and practiced for ten years before launching, with her husband, the *Georgia Gazette*, a small weekly paper that remarkably went on to win a Pulitzer Prize. They sold the paper for one dollar when its losses became too backbreaking to absorb. Scardino parlayed her experience running the *Gazette* into a top executive position at the *Economist's* North American operations, which at the time (in the late 1980s) could hardly be called operations. *Newsweek* and *Time* were at their peak then, and few people in the United States had even heard of the *Economist*, which was primarily written and produced in the UK.

Scardino and her team changed the magazine's trajectory. In the six years that she led the North American group, circulation in the United States more than doubled, from 100,000 to 230,000, which earned Scardino a promotion to manage worldwide business and in 1997 the chief executive job at Pearson. She was the first woman to head a FTSE 100 (Financial Times Stock Exchange 100 Index) company and the first American to run Pearson. Scardino inherited a company that was still a giant multinational but had lost its way—and, more important, its identity. Although its publications made Pearson a household name and a trusted institution in the UK, and increasingly around the world, the company also had its fingers in an incoherent array of other businesses: investment bankers Lazard, the unprofitable technology outfit Mindscape, and Madame Tussaud's waxworks, to name just a few.

Obviously, these extraneous parts of the company had to go. But that wouldn't be enough to get Pearson on track. After all, in the late 1990s media was experiencing the first tremors in the massive Web-based disruption that would permanently alter the way news is gathered and delivered. (the *New York Times*, for instance, began its online edition in 1996). Faced with this, Scardino directed a two-pronged strategy. First, isolate Pearson's institutional brand. What makes people trust Pearson; what are its core tenets? Second, reenergize Pearson's distinctive institutional character to be relevant in the new global environment.

The first part was relatively easy. At its heart, for nearly 150 years, Pearson was a provider of high-quality, accurate, and diligently developed content with an unbiased global perspective. That was what made Pearson distinctive and valuable. Scardino's challenge was to rebuild Pearson in that image, modernizing where needed, adding or subtracting as necessary. To amplify its content, Scardino acquired educational businesses that covered the gamut from testing services to academic publishing and executive education. At the same time, she pumped money into expanding the *Financial Times* and the *Economist* into global markets and onto electronic platforms and developed an early digital strategy to sell Pearson's products through multiple online channels. By the time her tenure atop Pearson was up in 2012, the firm was three times more profitable than when she first became CEO. Perhaps most important, the *Economist* had become one of the world's most trusted sources for unbiased and thorough news reporting.

An important thing happens when you define an institution's purpose in order to revive it: difficult questions about how to act and advance the institution so it remains relevant become clearer. The institution's core principles, in effect, become the framework for decision-making and the language for dialogue about how to proceed.

Step 2. Multilateral Organizations: (Re)design the Institution around a Fractured World

It would be hard for anyone to disagree with the observation that the world is a hopelessly divided place. People are worried about severe wealth inequality; disempowerment due to technological disruption; and online and physical social communities that serve as echo chambers to separate rather than unite us around reliable news and information. Everywhere you look, people are the less-than-proud recipients of the short end of the stick. In such an environment, the role of our institutions is to recognize the fears underlying the differences that bedevil us and be active participants in assuaging our worries. Our most critical institutions, however, have fallen well short in serving that function. In particular, and most disturbingly, institutions that we need to achieve cross-national and multilateral collaboration—the very institutions we need to address the worries raised by the ADAPT framework—are not at all prepared to be useful in a fractured world.

The German economics scholar Dennis Snower reached that conclusion in 2017, in a somewhat notable shift in his thinking that exposes the steep climb institutions have before them. Snower is widely respected around the world for a lifetime of work that in subject matter went well beyond the output of most economists, spanning the gamut of institutional, psychological, labor, and behavioral economics.[3] He was a devout globalist who had agreed for decades with the consensus that economic growth and social prosperity are linked and that integrated institutions were the foundation of global success.

But in 2017, when Snower was asked by the German government to prepare agenda items for an upcoming G20 summit in Hamburg, he realized that this yearly meeting of industrial nations—the world's most visible institution ostensibly focused on charting paths to progress for all nations to follow—was built around obsolete ideas. In recent years, he noted, many economies were recording steady growth of production and income but large segments of the population felt left behind. Their quality of life had worsened or become more precarious; in globalized economic markets they felt disempowered, stymied from shaping their own fate through their own efforts, and they were alarmed by the disintegration of their established communities. Jobs, wages, environmental conditions, housing, and education were deteriorating. Where, Snower wondered, was the social advancement that was supposed to accompany economic gains? In his words: "It is important to recognize that the underlying purpose of the G20 is to satisfy human needs worldwide, starting with the needs of the neediest people. Promoting economic growth and financial stability are simply means to an end."[4]

With that change of heart—with that statement of purpose chiding the G20 for not recognizing the fractured world they inhabited (and were responsible for)—Snower began the arduous effort to redesign the multilateral institution. He determined that to, as he put it, recouple economic and social progress, the way the discussion points for the annual summits were arrived at had to be fixed. Generally, from one year to the next, the leader of the host nation listed priority issues that they wanted to target at the meeting (usually economic and social issues they were interested in that affected their country) and a team of thinktanks called the T20 (the group that Snower was leading for the German G20) provided research-based policy advice for the agenda. That approach yielded a different set of topics each year without any consistent follow-up from one to the next to ensure that whatever the impact of the economic strategies put in place, the people who lived in the G20 were gaining the social benefits.

Snower's creative answer to this problem was to design a new entity in essence connected to the T20, called the Global Solutions Initiative (GSI). This group, made up of thinktanks and thought leaders, maintained an ongoing narrative of common global social problems that had to be covered by the G20 to adequately address the most pressing issues. This could also help the T20 become an intellectual backbone of the G20, augmenting the shaping of its agenda development. The GSI's initial narrative—that economic prosperity could become decoupled from social prosperity and that the job of the G20 was to recouple these differing sides of prosperity and focus on human well-being—became a guiding premise for the entire G20 labyrinth.[5] It allowed the T20 to nudge its superior, the G20, to not neglect pressing anxieties that individuals in each country felt in their day-to-day lives, and gave the G20 the flexibility it needed to cover the favored topics of the host.

It was an elegant solution crafted by Snower—and now going on three years, it has already been successful in changing the tenor and contours of the G20 meetings. Snower is soft-spoken so, at first blush, would not seem to be a person who could redirect one of the world's biggest institutions. But he accomplished this because of two somewhat contradictory qualities: he is a man of vast integrity, willing to recognize when a life's work of assumptions need to be challenged, even at the cost of being rejected by many of his German colleagues who disagreed with his new positions; and his mild-mannered demeanor backed by the depth of his intelligence allowed him to bring brilliant people with very diverse theories and points of view together around a common cause. That is especially noteworthy when you consider that most of the T20 members were initially committed to the G20's traditional focus on economic and financial policy, with only passing reference to social prosperity as a distinct goal.

As Snower's thinking about tackling global problems has evolved, he points to three observations. First, all of us have many identities, based on our hobbies, interests, race, religion, location, nation, city, favorite food—the list is virtually infinite. And there is a growing emphasis on the diversity of those identities among people in the world. Thus the notion that the nation-state is the preeminent source of our identities is far from inevitable. Second, countries are championing quite different views of the optimal version of a political economy. Third, with that said, there are still critical issues—surrounding trade, global finance, climate change, and the like—that require purposeful cooperation among all of us. Given this, Snower suggests that global governance should be rethought around layers of governing bodies, with challenges tackled at the most local level possible.[6] Every governance decision at any layer begins with the assumption that we live in a world with competing views about what is best and competing identities with competing demands. This is a radical departure from the belief in centralized global institutions dominated by top-heavy nation-states seeking broad consensus that has implicitly guided us for the past seventy years.

Snower's G20 plan for institutions to deal with global fissures applies of course most easily to big systems. But while the global economy has become more integrated, global societies and political systems have become more fragmented, and thus it will be increasingly important to address global problems through social, economic, and political changes that enable our multiple identities to complement, rather than compete with, one another. In education, focus first on the classroom. In policing, the neighborhood. In politics, the wards, precincts, and streets. In healthcare, preventive medicine and the well-being of individuals. Remain mindful that humans have always mastered their challenges through collaboration in small groups and that global solutions require small groups to be working in harmony with our national and international institutions.

Step 3. Education: Accelerate the Ability to Change

A repeated motif in this book has been that education as an institution is letting us down. From elementary and high schools to colleges and universities, many students are not sufficiently taught what they need to know to elevate themselves and prosper in a dynamically altering technological world and the best and most effective education is often reserved for a small group of individuals (a group actually becoming even smaller) that can afford elite schools. In other words, the value of education is rapidly being subsumed by the other disturbing global trends involving technology, demographic shifts, and social and economic disparity. The upshot is that education as an institution is in a sort of paralysis, caught in a maelstrom of external and self-inflicted pressures and unable to change or find a way out of its dilemma.

Not every educator is able to assess this situation with the appropriate clarity it needs to do something about this dilemma, but Jim Danko is one who undeniably does. I got to know Danko well during a hurricane in 1996, when he came down to interview for a position at Duke. The university shut down for three days, giving Jim and me a lot of time together to discuss the challenges of education as an institution and bandy back and forth realistic and totally fanciful solutions—while sharing ice cream we had to save from melting since due to the storm there was no electricity to his hotel refrigerator.

Fifteen years later, when Danko became president of Butler University, we once again colluded to fix university-level education. Danko had hit up against that most existential problem for institutions in the current global environment—too slow to change and thus at risk of becoming irrelevant. Butler was founded in 1855 with the mission that everyone deserved a great education regardless of race or color, a provocative idea in the pre–Civil War United States. Although the mission has modified slightly, Butler has always emphasized the need to provide accessible, high-quality education. It has been a hugely successful regional school consistently ranked the best in the Midwest.

But Danko was not satisfied with that; he is a peripatetic intellect who has that great quality for an educator of never thinking we know enough about answers we provide. He was wary that Butler was resting on its history and not transforming fast enough to provide students with the education that they needed in today's world. Three things bothered him the most: (1) universities weren't really preparing kids for the technology revolution; (2) universities were increasingly not managing the ongoing need for education as people continue through life postdegree; and (3) universities were contributing to economic and social inequities, evidenced by the fact that schools placing kids more effectively in the job market were more likely to recruit from wealthy families and they didn't make themselves known or available to places where the kids with the biggest needs for a great education lived. Instead, universities were recruiting from elite schools in every state, by and large neglecting good students from average schools.

In Danko's view these were deep-seated issues that had established themselves due to Butler's inherent conservatism. Institutions are lost in their own inertia, he thought, because they fail to comprehend that today's problems won't just resolve themselves over time; they were fundamental and new, and institutions had to disrupt themselves to fix them. To get this across to his board, Danko asked me to present the ADAPT framework to the group. He wanted me to lay out in stark detail the wellsprings of the crisis of prosperity and how technology was disrupting people's lives and threatening their jobs. He asked me to talk about the creeping peril of demographics and polarization and especially the palpable loss of trust in institutions, well-deserved because by inaction they were abdicating their positive role in society. "I need someone that they would consider credible to make this case deeper, harder, stronger than I would," Danko told me. "Paint the extreme picture of ADAPT. And I need you to talk about it in a way that it isn't just about the university, but about the dangers to the larger society."

Soon after I spoke to the board, Danko was able to get Butler's leadership to agree to an imaginative plan that has the potential to change the nature of the university, leaving its valuable traditional elements in place while providing a pathway for innovation and experimentation. The plan had three parts.

1. Fashion an alternative entity, attached to the university but outside its governance structure, that was designed to expedite the debut of new student programs, taking risks with fresh ideas, accepting that some will fail and then learning from that failure. Even the board could not deny that this wouldn't be possible within Butler's conventional channels for program development. It would tackle questions like, What does a lifelong learning model entail? Which less expensive undergraduate programs are worth trying out? What elements would a pure technology-based degree have? The notion was to create a structure that would permit much faster experimentation and implementation of new untried educational and lifelong learning concepts than is traditionally possible in a university, ultimately to accelerate the ability for a university to change while maintaining important aspects of governance that make our educational systems worthy of trust and essential

to our society. This part of the plan permitted the next two elements to occur.

2. Find new revenue streams, in areas such as executive education, alternative degree programs, and lifelong learning; if Butler didn't, undergraduate fees would continue to rise, boxing out anyone but the wealthiest students. Without the ability to raise endowments like Harvard, Yale, or Stanford, Butler could not afford to underwrite degree programs for a wide swath of students from less well-heeled communities. This portion of the strategy was engineered to use new degree options and pathways to allow greater access, employability, and affordability.

3. Enhance holistic student learning by focusing on the student experience throughout the twenty-four-hour day, linking curriculum, pedagogy, and programs to the needs of employers and expanding the number and range of high-impact practice opportunities. All of these elements were meant to help Butler fulfill its mission to offer accessible solutions for learners currently excluded from traditional private higher education. Just like before the Civil War, Butler is continuing its focus on access for all.

Step 4. Local First:
Community Connections

A principal reason why institutions have by and large failed and are not viewed as trustworthy anymore is that they have become estranged from the communities that they are supposed to serve. They no longer prove their value by their day-to-day presence in the community and the positive results of their activities. In today's landscape, that is a significant missed opportunity. With so many initiatives to address ADAPT concerns fitting into the category called Local First, the way established institutions directly support and enhance the development of these initiatives could determine their long-term success as well as the viability of the institutions themselves. Since institutional responsibilities include such a broad swath of societal activity, their potential impact in helping local communities and innovators design programs to tackle inequities, fears, and concerns cannot be overstated.

One person who understood some time ago the importance of the institution and the Local First relationship was Frederick Terman, the former provost of Stanford University and dean of the Engineering School, a man I count among my heroes.[7] I met him only once, shortly before he died in 1982, when I spoke with him about a topic that was in retrospect too big for one conversation: I wanted him to help me discover how a university could come to match the success of Stanford. What I received was a treatise on academic innovation that had at its heart an unforgettable message: the link between society and the university must be indestructible.

Terman was a brilliant man with a remarkably practical ability to break problems down into their simplest components to find uncomplicated solutions. When he became dean at Stanford just after World War II, Terman knew that he faced a tall order in trying to get funding from the Department of Defense and other government agencies that were supporting much of the engineering activity in the country. East Coast schools like MIT, Carnegie Mellon, Johns Hopkins, and Princeton were favored, while a university like Stanford in Palo Alto, a long way from Washington, DC, and New York, was at a distinct disadvantage.

To overcome this, Terman dedicated some of Stanford's unused land to establish an industrial park, the first owned by a university in the world. He convinced William Hewlett and David Packard, two of his graduate students, to house their new company there. Over the years as Stanford Industrial Park expanded, Terman led efforts to link the university financially to some of the start-ups that moved into the park—and before long there was a continuous line of Stanford graduates populating the site. Terman's initiative came to be known as Silicon Valley, a perfect example of an institution and a community embedded together for everyone's gain. It was a product of necessity. Today the necessity for institutions of all kinds to do the same thing in ways applicable to their roles could not be greater.

◎ ◎ ◎

The need to connect to the community should be a priority particularly for operational institutions that serve society directly—police forces, financial service firms, tax collectors, and healthcare providers, to name a few. When these types of institutions fail to be truly present in the communities they serve, serious harm can be done. In many communities these institutions are essential for local residents and the social network of the community to thrive. Thus the damage from the sustained failure of so many institutions to recognize the concerns of their local communities and to provide tangible answers cannot be overstated.

Leaders of all institutions could learn a tremendous amount from the principles and the leaders studied in this chapter. They all took imaginative, bold, intriguing, and risky steps, usually without fear, although not with total confidence. They adopted, each in ways that suited their situations, aspects of the four elements essential to protecting and reviving their institutions: (1) identify the institution's core principles and innovate around them; (2) design the institution's operations to survive and improve people's lives in a fractured world; (3) accelerate new ideas and their execution while not alienating those who fear change; and (4) forge intimate connections with the local community and the people to be served. Institutions are essential for a cohesive world; they are the glue that holds us together in big and small ways, in big and small regions—from across continents to a neighborhood. The crises identified in this book cannot be solved with broken institutions.

CHAPTER 10

Culture:
Refreshing Technology

Innovation as a Social Good

Recently, a cross-section of US residents was asked about their feelings toward some of the more highly publicized new technologies that are predicted to play a big role in the contours of the future. The results were less than flattering—if you are a piece of digital equipment, that is. According to the poll conducted by Pew Research, 73 percent of Americans are very or somewhat worried about a world in which robots and computers are capable of performing many human jobs, and 76 percent of respondents said that they believed automation of jobs would intensify economic inequality. A full 75 percent of respondents were skeptical that new, better-paying positions will be created for humans who lose their jobs to machines.[1]

Autonomous vehicles (AVs) fared only slightly better: 56 percent of Americans said they would never trust the technology enough to ride in one. Although one of the primary selling points of self-driving cars is that they will in time eliminate fatal vehicle accidents, as many as 30 percent of Pew respondents said that AVs would do the opposite—lead to an increase in road deaths.

These findings are not surprising when you consider that much of the new technology we are just beginning to get used to today comes with a very sharp double-edged sword. Some of it is already making the world a better place. The most important events in our lives—for instance, buying a home or a car or planning a wedding—as well as essential chores like shopping are simplified, made more convenient, and enhanced with a personal touch through customization. Information that once took hours or days to find is at our fingertips. The business models of slow-to-change, inefficient industries are being modernized and their assumptions questioned. Staying in touch with each other and our communities has never been easier.

Yet despite the obvious ways that technology serves us well, headlines consist of technology's unrelenting dark side: its impact on jobs and wealth, its intrusions on our privacy and political systems, the odd isolation that social media engenders, the disinformation channels that manipulate truth, online bullying, and more. The list is long and portends peril. Because of how readily we bring new technologies—hardware, software, platforms, and apps—into our lives (even as we fear them), the harm that they can visit upon us as individuals and citizens of global communities can be enormous and near permanent.

Urgently we have to make tough decisions about the way technology is implemented and used today. With appropriate thoughtfulness—dispassionately identifying the undesirable elements of technology and championing its advantages—our choices can lead to positive outcomes and mitigate the negative ones. We need to forge disciplines, practices, and policies to help people make those decisions smartly—and we have to protect each other from online retribution, reputational risk, or threats to our livelihoods if we attack the excesses of technology. Five steps can be taken immediately to rein in technology. They are fundamental but essential, including (1) upskilling for a digital world; (2) safeguarding data from misuse; (3) enhancing the role of civil society to help find solutions to privacy questions and better police technology; (4) setting controls on artificial intelligence; and (5) improving our personal behavior and controlling our appetites vis-à-vis technology.

We Can't Control Technology If We Don't Understand It

Technology is leaving a large number of us behind. On the one hand, there are those who are adept around platforms and apps or who have access to large amounts of cloud storage and various pieces of connected hardware to ingest information and quickly transform it into useable knowledge. These folks are in a better position than the second group of people, who are Luddites or otherwise do not have the wherewithal or the access to participate in the digital revolution.

This technology divide is a costly and unviable situation and can be ameliorated only by an enormous global upskilling campaign aimed at achieving three urgent goals. The first goal is ensuring that people everywhere are as future-proof as possible, minimizing employment disruption, particularly among aging populations, as jobs transition into requiring advanced digital skills. The second goal is allowing everyone to engage thoughtfully and intelligently in finding ways to humanize technology; the search for solutions to the excesses of technology must be citizen-led, while business and government leaders must participate. The third goal is beginning to reduce the knowledge, social, and economic gaps between the haves and have-nots, gaps that are expanding as technology increasingly drives these elements of daily life.

An upskilling effort of this magnitude and necessity can be achieved only with a *massive, fast campaign*. This effort can be broken down into these actions:

> *Building workforce capabilities*. Individuals in every region must obtain the minimum level of digital skills that are needed for jobs of today and tomorrow.

> *Amplifying digital understanding*. Leaders in the public and private sectors must have sufficient understanding of the potential harm that technology can do as well as sensitivity to the fears that global residents harbor about technology. Without that, they cannot play a

role in driving technology for the public good and leading technology-propelled organizations effectively. In addition, citizens around the world must grasp technology well enough to participate in managing it and in holding their leaders accountable.

> *Help the have-nots.* Find and train people currently excluded from the opportunities that technology offers because they opted out or live in places that are digitally disadvantaged.

Targeting these actions requires that the case for upskilling be made and agreed upon globally. Ongoing sharing of intellectual property and best practices in the name of conceiving a digitally prepared global populace is necessary. Moreover, at the local and regional levels a governance structure for the upskilling campaign must be drawn up that includes clear definitions of priorities, strategies for addressing these priorities, funding channels, partnerships, and capabilities needed to train and retrain a large group of people. And perhaps most important, there must be concerted and large-scale engagement from the private sector; governments and civil society are important, but without private sector buy-in the training efforts would not be focused on the types of skills needed for people to retain jobs during digital disruption, nor would they be financially secure enough.

We Have a Data Dilemma

Information, especially personal information, is both a public and private good. In various forms—that is, anonymized or as a component of statistics or even as raw data—big data pools of individual habits and preferences, health histories and shopping records, information accessed, and what we read are extremely valuable. These data pools help companies use technology for positive outcomes, delivering efficient and customizable services, catalyzing breakthroughs in, for instance, medical equipment and pharmaceuticals and giving us more hours in the day for leisure and things to do with this free time. Equally important, though, is that personal and sensitive data about each of us is protected from public distribution or misuse by corporations or governments.

Some parts of the world take that mission very seriously. Since the end of World War II, Europe has led the way in legislating strong privacy protections for data about individuals and their activities. The latest EU regulations require companies to get permission from European customers before collecting their personal data. The United States has lagged in this—just look at how much private information Facebook secretly hoovers up and turns into a revenue stream. And Asian countries are even worse in this regard. While data privacy legislation is necessary, the private sector—and particularly the leaders of major technology companies—must be in the forefront in finding and implementing solutions that safeguard the trillions of pieces of personal information generated by hundreds of millions of customers and clients. Although many technology executives claim to be sympathetic to data protection concerns, few seem to be actually backing it up with action.

One CEO who deserves credit for at least moving his very large company in the right direction is Microsoft's Satya Nadella. Only the third chief of Microsoft, after Bill Gates and Steve Ballmer, Nadella was born in Hyderabad, India, and got his master's in electrical engineering at the University of Wisconsin–Milwaukee. Nadella has set Microsoft on a new mission: where company cofounder Gates hoped for "a PC on every desk and in every home, running Microsoft software," Nadella wants to "empower every person and every organization on the planet to achieve more."[2]

As part of this goal, Nadella believes that data privacy is a "human right" and has vowed that Microsoft will not monetize customers' personal data or use it for profit. His cloud computing strategy is a window into his thinking on this topic. The centerpiece of this offering is separating public from private data. Microsoft's cloud servers would store and manage the nonsensitive data that reveals nothing about the identity of its subjects or where it came from, while each client's local servers, accessible only to the companies themselves, would maintain and protect private data. In other words, when a client wants to use Microsoft's cloud-based analytical tools, it extracts data from its private servers, forgets where it came from, performs the analysis on the cloud, and then ships those results back to its private servers. All of this is accomplished virtually instantaneously; otherwise the cost of the transaction in time would make private server–public cloud technology too slow.

There are other alternatives being considered as well to address the data protection issue. One of the more prominent ones recently has been blockchain, which essentially turns every data transaction into a series of anonymized blocks. The transaction can be verified and tracked at every stage but cannot be decoded and the individuals initiating the communication hold private keys that allow them to control how the information is used and who is allowed to view it. Blockchain is an attractive idea that has a lot of merit, although there are crucial issues to work out. For instance, how do you make it reversible? You may want to call the interaction off and erase it totally, but at this stage you can't do that even though that's a necessary component of data protection as well. Another question involves figuring out how to make some of the data in the blockchain public but only for a short period of time and for a specific use.

Today's alternatives will likely look primitive in a few years. But whatever solutions we arrive at must address the public–private information problem head-on, in a manner completely divorced from the current massive, centralized data farms that serve as the basis of most information and economic exchanges today.[3]

Where Is Civil Society?

To help institute controls on platforms like Facebook, Google, Amazon, and Baidu, and to control the proliferation of artificial intelligence and its impact on our social structures, civil society—technology-focused organizations, NGOs, nonprofits—must play a part in helping determine who controls new technology and what rules and social norms are needed to protect society from it. These civil society organizations will have to be given access to the resources, both data and financial, to allow them to do so. We need to find a way to strengthen the role of civil society and provide equivalent resources to research and development with a primary focus on crafting AI and platforms with people at the heart of the solution.

So what might that look like? One solution is to provide equivalent access to data for those whose primary interest is the creation of public goods. A pool (or, in cloud parlance, a lake) of information and access to resources for those who have clearly passed the standard of a legitimate not-for-profit organization. A few principles should hold for those wishing to access resources or information in civil society. All results should be made available in the public domain, personal information has to be protected with state-of-the-art cybersecurity and data-masking protocols, and governance practices of the type discussed below need to be in place. Organizations wishing to be considered should have to go through some form of peer review by academics and informed citizens to determine the types of access provided to data and the level of funding. Providing funding for this type of initiative will of course be a key part of the solution. One answer might be that platforms are required to put aside a fund for this.

How Can You Govern What You Can't See?

As noted in chapter 3, we are about to enter a world in which artificial intelligence plays an increasingly dominant role and we aren't close to understanding how AI programs learn and what their responses will be to new commands or programming inputs. We don't comprehend how AI software develops biases toward some items or language or characteristics of individuals and how its reactions reflect the unique realities that it embodies. To most of us, the way AI programs analyze new information is still fairly alien, opaque, and sometimes even random. Because of these features, even well-intended AI-based solutions could have seriously harmful consequences and we may not know it until it's too late.

Despite these unpredictable outcomes, AI has huge potential. It could add $15.7 trillion into the global economy by 2030, with the greatest economic gains in China and North America. But while we rush headlong into the era of artificial intelligence, another PwC study found that only 25 percent of executives surveyed would consider prioritizing the ethical implications of an AI solution before investing in it.[4] That's not a promising statistic. Business and governmental leaders cannot abrogate their responsibility for the consequences of artificial intelligence and must work toward building an ethical AI environment focusing on these five primary dimensions:

1. Establish effective governance across all elements of AI strategy, planning, ecosystem (internal and external players in a project), development, deployment, operations, and measurement. These questions should be addressed: Who is accountable for each facet of an AI implementation? How does AI align with the business strategy? What processes could be modified to improve the outputs and make them less opaque? What controls need to be in place to track performance and identify problems? Are the results consistent and reproducible?

2. Create a set of practical, frontline-relevant principles for ethical AI practice, educate everyone involved, and hold them accountable for applying those principles. In instances of organizational culture change, such as the development of whole new principles, leadership from the top is essential.

3. Insist on the development of transparent artificial intelligence—that is, AI whose data sources and decision rules can be inspected, debated, and adjusted in response to legitimate concerns from thoughtful reviewers.

4. Design AI systems that are robust and secure. That means the AI program is sufficiently self-reflective so that it can correct faulty decisions quickly with adjustments to its core algorithms. In addition, it should be drawn up in such a manner that a flaw in visualizing or understanding

an idea, expression, statement, or something in a physical space would not cause serious harm. In other words, no autonomous vehicle should be on the road if there is any chance that it could misread a stop sign and instead go full speed through a busy intersection.

5. Root out as much as possible bias from AI systems. Recently reported cases of AI programs exhibiting racial bias in the criminal justice realm and gender discrimination in hiring were disconcerting. Of course, all decisions ultimately entail disappointing some people to the benefit of others. In each case, companies, managers, or individuals must balance the choices they make against the harm that these choices cause and to whom. However, hopefully these decisions are not clouded by unfair or unethical biases. Similarly, with an AI system, developers and anyone responsible for managing these programs must be extremely mindful of tuning the technology to mitigate bias and enable decisions that are as fair as possible and that adhere to an organization's code of ethics as well as antidiscrimination regulations.

Unfortunately, we are unlikely to make the investments necessary to implement these five AI protective dimensions as long as the vast majority of executives do not believe we need to. Perhaps the way to begin to change that attitude is by approaching an AI development project with this question: What if it was my family member, friend, colleague, community, or organization that was inadvertently seriously harmed by the unforeseen consequences of the AI system that I am responsible for?

We Need to Learn How to Behave Ourselves

While technophobia is a real thing and nearly every survey about technology adoption reveals a rippling undertow of fear about new hardware and software, we can't seem to resist buying the stuff or jumping onto every platform that glides across our screens. We are seemingly well aware of the ability of social media to divide and mislead us and increase our ambient anxiety or of tablets and phones to distract and compel us to respond immediately to text messages, email, and other alerts, pulling us away from what we should be doing often against our better judgment and to the detriment of our well-being.[5] Yet we are unable to resist the allure of these shiny new technologies.

Because these technologies are such a recent phenomenon and so different from what we have experienced before, we cannot draw on earlier research conducted about the impact on people of media like TV or radio or even the early versions of the Internet to help us determine how to develop good habits, create smart policies and laws, or derive appropriate practices and safeguards for using and integrating this technology. Given that vacuum of information, it is imperative that we now study quickly, carefully, and honestly how a platform-based, machine-filled world is affecting individuals, communities, organizations, and governments.

Some of the best initial analysis in this area has come from University of California at San Francisco neuroscience professor Adam Gazzaley, whose work with Cal State psychology professor Larry Rosen was highlighted in chapter 3. Among the solutions that Gazzaley offers to alter our technology-obsessive behavior is the use of technology itself to help mitigate its negative impact. To demonstrate this, Gazzaley developed a game called NeuroRacer, a three-dimensional interactive program in which players steer a car up a treacherous hilly road with their left thumb, while watching for signs of specific shapes and colors that they must shoot down with their right thumb. The mixture of essential cognitive skills required to play NeuroRacer well—such as the ability to focus attention on two things at once and to use temporary memory to hold on to multiple pieces of information for immediate recollection—appear to improve neuroplasticity and the facility to filter out distractions.[6]

In addition, Gazzaley and others have stressed the importance of developing new habits and disciplines to not only neutralize the negative consequences of technology on cognition but to enhance our ability to function in a in a world in which technology is ubiquitous. One of the more charming examples of new behaviors is the growing practice of young adults to stack their cell phones in the center of a table during dinner or other social gatherings. The person who can't resist the vibrating phones any longer and looks at their device first picks up the tab for everyone. Other suggestions include partitioning your day into separate designated times for work, social networking, answering emails, and browsing the Web so that the technology doesn't become a constant interrupter; frequent breaks during which you get away from technology and spend a few minutes outside; or even ten minutes every few hours when you can daydream, nap, or meditate without distractions.

◎ ◎ ◎

We all need to be good students of technology and its impact on society and ourselves. To take on this task responsibly and effectively, we need to have a somewhat paradoxical mindset; we need to be what I call *tech-savvy humanists*. That is, we must understand both what people require from technology to make their lives better as well as the full breadth of technology's potential to alter the world around us in big and small ways. The problem with merely being an astute student of people and human systems is that, in a technology-driven world, you are irrelevant. However, if you are a tech whiz in a world of people, you could do real harm. Ideally the path to developing tech-savvy humanists would begin in elementary school.

As we seek to implement the solutions proposed in this chapter, we will need to do massive things fast on a global scale and adopt personal behavioral changes as well. A fractured world makes the larger answers harder to implement, but with technology increasingly dominating our existence—a trend that will accelerate in the coming years—the option to do nothing is not viable.

CHAPTER 11

Massive and Fast: Problems That Cannot Wait

With our institutions in disarray and mired in dysfunction, only a few of them—led by extraordinary individuals with unique leadership skills—will be able to address the global, national, and local challenges that must be remedied quickly (greater than ten years is too long) and at enormous scale. These problems are so big and so urgent that we cannot wait for our institutions to catch up, especially because corralling these crises requires entirely new and imaginative approaches. Clearly, our institutions, as we know them today, are not up to that task.

But while all of the crises covered in this book cannot be seen as anything but acute, a few enormous problems emerging stand out as more dire and pressing than the others. I call these problems *massive, fast* challenges. They are huge and seem intractable—and we need massive change, fast, to mitigate them. Time is of the essence and to solve these challenges, global or regional collaboration as well as public–private sector cooperation is required.

Two Global Crises

Two global challenges stand out as undeniably massive, desperately pressing, and badly in need of creative solutions as well as focused and concerted attention from countries around the world. They are the dire challenges of lost jobs and climate change. Let's look at job losses first.

If we take the conservative estimate that 10 percent of jobs in the world will be eliminated over the next ten years by automation technology, we would need to retrain and find positions for three hundred million people currently in the workforce. To add to this challenge, there are more than one billion youth under twenty years old living in underdeveloped countries who need education now and a job in the next ten years. If we do not address this challenge immediately, the likely consequences are dire. Consider the worsening impact of these job losses on wealth disparities for future generations across the globe. And then consider what tens of millions of young people with no obvious future, falling behind other more fortunate people in their societies, will do in response. They will migrate en masse, revolt, start wars. One thing they won't do is be positive forces in their countries, adding to the potential for innovation and lifestyle improvements that every region badly needs. While this essentially class conflict plays out, a dangerous situation could take root in which smart, pervasive technology would be embedded with people largely unaware of its potential benefits and harms.

Next, let's consider the global crisis of climate change. Estimates of the effects of global warming suggest we have little more than a decade to dramatically modify our carbon footprint before things are potentially irreversible.[1] Flooding, drought, and intense summer heat as well as violent storms could become the new normal. Drastic changes in global water supplies could severely compromise global health, availability of food, and fragile ecosystems. From today's vantage point—looking at the lack of political will, the attacks on scientific facts coming from some quarters, and the hot and cold conflicts that separate nations—it is hard to imagine that we can summon up a global effort to stall climate change.

Few would argue that either of these global crises lack the utmost urgency. The challenge of lost jobs involves the nature of migration and the unimaginable consequences of enormous numbers of people being unemployed on a global basis—how that would foment perilous political upheaval and further fracturing of relationships within and among nations everywhere. The challenge of climate change is, simply put, an existential threat for humanity and the natural world. Both crises beg for massive, fast solutions.

But beyond the obvious need for massive, fast approaches to these problems is something particularly compelling and essential. At a time of impenetrable political and social disagreements and global fissures, spreading populist movements, economic dysfunction and disillusionment, technological fears and uncertainty, institutional malaise and imminent demographic warfare, problems that affect everyone like global unemployment and natural destruction from climate change are also galvanizing bonds for all of us. They are enemies at all of our gates; enemies we have in common. And what we need now, in fact, are common enemies of exactly this type, enemies that bring us closer together through our shared efforts to solve and eliminate enormous problems. Left alone, these crises will tear us further apart and render us all helpless.

Indeed, massive, fast programs, by their very nature—specifically their size and scale—address each of the universal worries raised in the ADAPT framework. They provide us with valuable experience and skills that we can use to accelerate our efforts in finding solutions to all of the crises we are compelled to withstand. Examples of success can inspire us to keep going. More granularly, massive, fast campaigns support the development and intensification of the strategies, structure, and cultural elements (the three sides of the change triangle) discussed earlier in the book. Amplifying while speeding up the potential impact of these three elements is essential to overcoming the welter of crises we face.

As it turns out, this is a particularly good moment for massive, fast solutions. Significant financial resources are obviously necessary for a global massive, fast effort, and in developed economies plenty of capital is now available for investment in these types of urgent global improvement activities. As evidence of the deep capital pools, interest rates are at or below zero in parts of Europe and at bare minimum levels in the United States. Using these funds for massive, fast programs would instantly provide substantial employment opportunities around the world, not to mention improve individual well-being and tamp down demographic and other social conflicts. But before those types of investments can be counted on, large global bankers will have to recraft their role and become the starting point for international innovative solutions to big problems, which in time will generate sufficient returns, encouraging other investors to add their funds to the mix.

National and Regional Challenges

While lost jobs and climate change are global in nature, urgent problems at the national or regional level deserve similar massive, fast attention. These crises could also benefit from strategic and tactical advances made in global massive, fast efforts and might gain in shared resources from the collaborative relationships begun during the massive, fast effort. As a starting point, consider this amalgam of serious challenges for countries around the world:

1. Heading off the pending retirement crisis in the United States.

2. Finding a solution to the significant tax challenges confronting Europe.

3. Creating opportunities for people in Russia living outside of Moscow and Saint Petersburg.

4. Addressing the educational and job creation needs of youth in Africa.

5. Creating a positive direction for the UK and the European Union after Brexit.

6. Solving the intergenerational disparity challenge in Australia.

7. Dealing with the environmental crisis in China.

It is tempting to dismiss the notion that in today's environment we could join together in a massive, fast effort. But optimistically, I prefer to characterize *massive, fast* as a dormant rather than a lost skill. After all, we *have* moved hugely and quickly before in an effort so imposing that it altered the trajectory of the world: the post–World War II Marshall Plan. Referencing the Marshall Plan can be instructive for us today because, like now, the world was fractured in the immediate aftermath of the war. Perhaps the Marshall Plan's most exemplary result was to initiate broad and strong social, political, and economic alliances that lasted upwards of seventy years in the non-Communist segment of the globe.

For that reason, it is worth keeping in mind the critical factors behind the Marshall Plan's success as we think about engaging in projects that are meant to solve massive problems fast. Columbia University economist Glen Hubbard identified four such factors.[2] First, there was a very clear global and local governance structure over the money, made possible by the existence of a single source of funding (that is, the United States). Second, there was notable engagement from the private sector; indeed, private sector growth was the target of the plan. Third, there were associated reforms by each government receiving support. Fourth, the regional coordinating body ensured that there was competition for funds; countries had to want the money and have a plan for how to use it.

Inside GAME

Obviously, there is not a single one-size-fits-all program for massive, fast efforts. However the Marshall Plan's uniquely successful approach is a good foundation for any large-scale challenge that we tackle today. One of the endeavors now under way that clearly follows the Marshall Plan's gleanings (intentionally or not) and addresses critical ADAPT framework concerns is a massive, fast solution called GAME.[3] First, the scope (spoiler alert, it is ambitious): the Global Alliance for Mass Entrepreneurship has the audacious mandate of supporting the development of ten million successful, local entrepreneurs in India by 2030, split equally between men and women. These entrepreneurs would start and run small and medium-sized businesses that would ultimately employ dozens, if not thousands, of people in every community. To put that aspiration in perspective, there are 5.6 million organizations with more than one hundred employees in the United States.

That's a big and stunningly speedy goal for a new organization, but GAME (which is just now getting off the ground) has the advantage of having the right person spearheading it. Ravi Venkatesan, GAME's founder and chairman, was formerly head of Microsoft and Cummins in India, leading the effort to give both of those multinationals a deep foothold in India. Subsequently, as chairman of Baroda Bank, Venkatesan headed up a campaign that transformed Baroda from a sleepy, bureaucratically bound state-owned firm into an agile, privately owned financial services outfit, India's second largest, with tentacles in every major money capital around the world. All of this is evidence that Venkatesan understands well how to build and manage large, global organizations in local surroundings from smaller beginnings.

For Venkatesan, GAME is the answer to the enormous jobs problem that India and Africa (GAME intends to expand into Africa once the India program is under way) face because it is the countervailing idea to a series of current trends that taken together will only continue to worsen the employment challenge. First, only 21 percent of India's nonagricultural jobs come from small to medium-sized enterprises, whereas in China that number is 83 percent, in Bangladesh it is 75 percent, and in the United States it is 53 percent. In other words, India (and Africa as well) is deficient in crucial business segments that create a lot of jobs. Second, large organizations in these regions are narrowly focused on increasing productivity to compete and hence on reducing the total number of people they employ. Automation and other IT initiatives in the coming years will accelerate this bias. Moreover, urban-based technology companies in India and Africa, such as the many outsourcing operations and global customer care lines, will never address employment needs for the vast majority of people who live in villages or small towns. And third, on the other side of the coin, there aren't enough opportunities for single-person firms in rural areas to make a dent in employment needs.

Ask Venkatesan about the states where GAME is piloting its efforts and he can describe in detail the failed grand initiatives to impose top-down, large-scale job creation. Those initiatives didn't work because in some cases they lacked sufficient commitments from the private sector or were slowed by too much red tape or were too management-heavy to operate close to the ground in small, close-knit communities. Yet in those same places, Venkatesan notes, there is still a large unmet demand for the kinds of services small and midsized entrepreneurial firms provide that meet basic human needs. These companies include hairdressers, specialized retailers, hotels, and restaurants. As these businesses grow from small operations into midsized entrenched local outfits, they hire additional workers, which expands the pool of potential customers for these businesses. This virtuous circle improves the regional economy and furthers job prospects.

This type of job creation strategy would be difficult enough to execute in a single community or region, let alone essentially over two continents, but Venkatesan has simplified the complexity of this massive, fast project with three inverse foundational principles that propel his plan forward: (1) it has a global vision that is local at its core; (2) it involves marshaling a big organization—complete with governance structures, task forces, and accountability and measurement systems, designed to encourage, enable, and support small and midsized businesses via individual entrepreneurs; and (3) it is based on a strategy that is vast in scope and speed but with almost painfully methodical and specified executional plans. Let's take a closer look at these three foundational principles:

1. *Global vision/local core.* Insight and learning from across the world about required skills, technology, and tools for entrepreneurship to blossom are rechanneled to local communities, forging an efficient system to accumulate knowledge globally and deliver it to individuals that can make best use of it in their home regions. The goal is to construct very different

value chains of capabilities development and technology needs as well as financing and market support tools in each GAME locale but to have the same broad pool of information and resources available to enhance these value chains. The starting point, support requirements, and skills deficits for each entrepreneur will be very different from place to place and person to person.

A primary obstacle is to change local mindset from the nearly exclusive pursuit of jobs in the public sector and large organizations to one in which entrepreneurship is viewed as an equally admirable career option. GAME hopes to adopt this way of thinking by globally nurturing entrepreneurial spirit and capabilities through India's and Africa's education systems, converting job seekers into entrepreneurs, teaching single entrepreneurs and microfirms how to scale their businesses for greater revenue and increasing the proportion of women who start and thrive as entrepreneurs.

2. *A big, well-funded organization encouraging entrepreneurship one person at a time.* A key insight that Venkatesan plucked from studying other attempts at developing entrepreneurs at scale was that they tended to be project-based, tactical efforts without sufficient capital or a muscular organizational structure designed to allow the operation to last for a long period of time. By contrast, GAME's underlying organization is impressive in its scope, resources, and capabilities. It includes alliance partners drawn from government, private sector, NGOs, implementation organizations, nonprofits, and donors, each of whom is thoroughly screened and brings skills necessary to execute on GAME's overall strategy; a set of task forces spearheaded by these partner organizations focused on each element of the GAME plan, from building the entrepreneurial mindset in schools to creating entrepreneurship models for each locale; and a separate team to support the task forces and help build the ecosystems essential to making the program work and endure. These organizational components are targeted at encouraging, developing, launching,

and supporting entrepreneurs one by one within a local business market and environment.

3. *Massive scope and speed but methodical plans.* When I first discussed GAME with Venkatesan, I was flabbergasted by the breadth of its goals (ten million entrepreneurs in India by 2030) and the extraordinary level of detail that he mustered in planning the organization. Glancing at his organizational map, I see that GAME is set up like a well-oiled machine, with interlocking parts and plenty of checks and balances. There are five sought outcomes, from nurturing entrepreneurial mindset early to turning job seekers into entrepreneurs to enabling women entrepreneurs; four targeted breakthroughs expected to be the backbone for vast scale, including advances in technology and frameworks for expanding capital and consumer markets; and eight task forces designed around the breakthroughs to identify innovations to work on further, mobilize and help fund local partners, and drive action at the local level. And this is just a thumbnail sketch of the depth of GAME's organizational structure that will serve as a platform for top-down, bottom-up economic development.

Big, complex projects with remarkable degrees of scale are hard to plan for in exquisite detail. Yet GAME does. Venkatesan recognizes that it is essential to be flexible and learn as things change, thus some details will undoubtedly be abandoned the first time a new and better lesson is gleaned. His approach is very much like a field marshal who has prepared the troops with thoroughness and diligence so they can navigate the uncertainties of not just a single battle but the whole war.

As noted, GAME's operating model closely mirrors many of the essential elements of the Marshall Plan that made it successful. Thus it serves well as a blueprint for other massive, fast projects. To wit:

1. GAME has a well-designed global and local governance structure managing money and other essential resources.

2. GAME has significant engagement from the private sector; indeed, private sector growth is the target of the plan.

3. GAME requires associated ecosystem adaptations in each locale receiving support.

4. GAME's regional strategy and place-based models ensure there is competition for support; locales need to want entrepreneurship as a core part of their success.

Like the Marshall Plan before it, GAME is entirely consistent with the worldview presented in this book to address global crises. It is Local First; it measures success by interdependence and inclusivity; it focuses on reshaping institutions—in particular, education and financial systems and local development organizations; and it uses technology beneficially to serve human needs.

To these elements, Venkatesan adds two more, which upon closer inspection also were prevalent in the Marshall Plan: learn before scaling and have enough capital to be patient with the projects in the portfolio, giving them sufficient time to evolve, gain a rhythm, and mature.

Of course, there are also differences between GAME and the Marshall Plan and they are equally important. In the Marshall Plan there was a single source of funding and implementation, the US government, but GAME will rely on a much wider support structure: private individuals lending money and talent, corporations providing expertise, local and national governments changing regulations and practices, and school systems altering curricula, just to name a few. The Marshall Plan was primarily designed to rearm economies along the lines that existed before the war, while GAME entails a dramatic change in thinking about how an economy should be built, how entrepreneurs are fostered, and how small and midsized businesses can spur economic growth in India and Africa. Finally, unlike the Marshall Plan, GAME does not implement and distribute projects and resources directly but works through alliance partners.

The Inevitability of Regional Solutions

Although the jobs shortage is a global dilemma—not restricted by any
means to developing countries—GAME is a regional answer. There is a
good reason for that, having to do with the decline of the nation-state as
the predominant identity for many people around the world—and with
that the lessening ability of nations to join together and solve problems as
a global force.

In 1993, Japanese organizational management specialist Kenichi Ohmae,
former dean of UCLA's Luskin School of Public Affairs, wrote about the
waning influence of nations, anticipating that conceptually countries would
be increasingly eclipsed by regional governing entities.[4] His argument was
based on two factors: first, many nations (most notably European but also
African and Caribbean countries) had given up control of their currency,
a crucial factor for economic unity within a nation; and second, most
nation-states were generally not natural economic units anyway, because
of the vast disparities within countries. Ohmae's primary example was how
little in common northern Italy had with southern Italy. But today he could
just as reasonably point to northern England and London, central China
and coastal China, or Uttar Pradesh and Bangalore. Ohmae predicted that
not only would regions become more meaningful political and economic
actors, but that they would begin to organize themselves across borders.
Indeed, today's massive, fast projects tend to punctuate the enhanced role
that regions are playing.

A lot of these regional solutions are popping up in Africa, where massive,
fast campaigns are sorely needed. Perhaps the one that best exemplifies the
declining relevance of national interests in favor of regional cooperation is
a new project called Smart Africa. Paul Kagame, Rwanda's president since
2000, is considered an unrelenting force by most who meet him. He led the
victorious insurgency that, in 1994, ended the genocide of Rwandan Tutsis
by Hutu extremists. Although it is undeniable that Kagame has strongman
tendencies (and reasonable critics who appropriately draw attention to

that aspect of his record), he has focused laserlike on bringing Rwanda into the twenty-first century and transforming it into a middle-income country. From a broader perspective, Kagame's most impressive accomplishment is Smart Africa, for which he has organized twenty-six disparate African countries into a coherent unit whose goal is to develop a single technology infrastructure for the continent as a means of advancing regional economies—and, with it, giving Africa control over its future.

Smart Africa's most audacious ambition is to digitally connect every individual, business, and government within Africa by 2030.[5] The project hopes to support local development of infrastructure, capital availability, financial and corporate regulations, and social planning to take advantage of the new digital capacity and rapidly advancing economies throughout Africa. It is entirely possible that this cross-border regional cooperative initiative could produce something not seen in the world; a multinational Sovereign Development Fund. In a nod to President John F. Kennedy, Kagame and his fellow leaders involved in Smart Africa have called this enterprise "Africa's Moonshot."

That is an apt metaphor for any massive, fast effort. Kennedy's challenge to the United States to send a man to the moon within a decade was inspiring and, ultimately, wildly rewarding—and a perfect example of what a nation, region, or globe can achieve when people (in the largest sense of the word) rally behind an endeavor. Not only did the United States win the physical race to the moon, but in the process the country elevated the stature of democratic systems compared with their communist rivals and became the world leader in science in ways that benefited the United States in the public and private arenas for years to come.[6] Millions of jobs were created over the years that could be linked directly or indirectly to going to the moon, many of them tied up in the list of spinoff technologies from the space race that could fill a book—including GPS systems, CT scans, wireless headsets, LED lighting, freeze-dried foods, memory foam, portable computers, scratch-resistant eyeglass lenses, mobile phones, water purification systems, and home insulation, to name just a few.[7]

Climate Change Needs Global Action

We need a similarly inspiring vision on a global scale if we are going to overcome the climate change crisis. Global massive, fast projects have shown to be nearly impossible to successfully implement, but climate change demands just that. Indeed, the climate crisis presents the perfect opportunity for leaders from government, business, and civil society or anyone else, such as a precocious sixteen-year-old from Sweden who so captivated the world with her passion about the issue in 2019, to come together on today's version of a moonshot. There are definite similarities: there is a clear enemy; as Kennedy had the Soviet Union and its lead in the space race, we have an unsustainable planet. Like then, there is evidence we are behind. Solving climate change will require collaboration across all elements of society and may reward us with substantial derivative innovation, new forms of work, and untold employment opportunities. And we have just ten years to complete the undertaking.

The elements of how a global effort to fight climate change could be mobilized today—an undertaking that would include contributions from governments as well as individuals, businesses as well as nonprofits, scientists as well as laypeople—are actually relatively easy to enumerate. Unfortunately this means that our lack of political will or collaboration skills may be the real enemy. These elements can be broken down into four categories.

First, we have to recognize the ways that we as a global society can dramatically reduce our carbon footprint *right now*. Although reducing the use of fossil fuels is crucial, there are many other possibilities that, if adopted as global priorities, could also have a surprisingly extraordinary impact. The most comprehensive analysis of what should be done to reverse global warming immediately is contained in a book called *Drawdown* by environmentalist Paul Hawken.[8] Among the one hundred possible actions and their carbon footprint reductions that Hawken delineates are some surprising entries. Next to the obvious options, like solar farms and geothermal energy, Hawken gives us family planning, plant-rich diets, and educating girls, to name but a few. Each solution in *Drawdown* has a significant impact on carbon emissions, is business-friendly (although some would greatly disrupt certain sectors but replace them with new industries and companies), and entails actions by all of us. His solutions have the potential to help address elements of other pressing crises described in this book, including creating more jobs and reducing economic asymmetry, tearing down nationalist walls, and rekindling trust in technology and institutions. For a summary of the actions we can take and the impact they would have, see Table 11.1.

The second essential element for establishing a global massive, fast plan to fight climate change is a recognition that we are already living with the dire effects of global warming—and they pale against what people will experience by 2030. Today, we are grudgingly getting used to enormous deadly storms and fires; severe declines in agricultural productivity; droughts; and extensive property losses. While we work to solve the problem of greenhouse gas in the atmosphere in the future, we need to have smart solutions for mitigating its impact today.

The third element for establishing a global, fast response is that we must encourage—with resources, development programs, education, and training—the rapid development of new technological solutions for global warming. Hawken provides some known technological answers, but what about the unknown ones yet to be discovered?

Finally, although our institutions do not appear to be up to the task of solving big, weighty problems—in fact, too often their shortcomings are part of the reason for these problems—we must include in any global climate crisis project the institutions that have the enlightened leadership and constituencies to be a positive force in the campaign. At some point we will need our core institutions to again play a central (and trustworthy) role in maintaining stability and fostering a sense of certainty in our lives as local, regional, and global citizens. If our institutions do not have a part in fixing global warming, they will be a major and disconcerting source of inertia.

TABLE 11.1 Top twenty actions to reduce our carbon footprint

	Solution	Sector	*Gigatons CO$_2$ Equivalent Reduced / Sequestered (2020–2050)*
1	Onshore Wind Turbines	Electricity	147.72
2	Utility-Scale Solar Photovoltaics	Electricity	119.13
3	Reduced Food Waste	Food, Agriculture, and Land Use / Land Sinks	94.56
4	Plant-Rich Diets	Food, Agriculture, and Land Use / Land Sinks	91.72
5	Health and Education	Health and Education	85.42
6	Tropical Forest Restoration	Land Sinks	85.14
7	Improved Clean Cookstoves	Buildings	72.65
8	Distributed Solar Photovoltaics	Electricity	68.64
9	Refrigerant Management	Industry / Buildings	57.75
10	Alternative Refrigerants	Industry / Buildings	50.53
11	Silvopasture	Land Sinks	42.31
12	Peatland Protection and Rewetting	Food, Agriculture, and Land Use / Land Sinks	41.93
13	Tree Plantations (on Degraded Land)	Land Sinks	35.94
14	Perennial Staple Crops	Land Sinks	31.26
15	Temperate Forest Restoration	Land Sinks	27.85
16	Managed Grazing	Land Sinks	26.01
17	Tree Intercropping	Land Sinks	24.40
18	Concentrated Solar Power	Electricity	23.96
19	Public Transit	Transportation	23.36
20	Regenerative Annual Cropping	Food, Agriculture, and Land Use / Land Sinks	22.27

©2020 Project Drawdown. Source: www.drawdown.org.
Under Project Drawdown Scenario 2, which stops climate change close to 1.5°C of global warming.

Technology as a Global Facilitator

One development, nonexistent at the turn of the twentieth-first century, that could make global campaigns to tackle global crises more possible is social media, with its unique and enormous reach and capability to rally large groups of people around a movement. No recent effort is more illustrative of this than the Arab Spring in late 2011 and beyond. Interestingly, I got a sneak preview of the Arab Spring and how social media would help drive it four months before it occurred, when I accompanied a global MBA class to the United Arab Emirates. In one of our sessions, Mohamed al Thani, a member of the royal family of Qatar, made a strikingly prescient set of observations to our group. He told us that emergent but limited new freedoms in the Gulf countries and Egypt would lead to a desire for more, and that the region's relatively young populations were getting extremely impatient with the current leadership and upset at the wealth disparity between people in power and everyone else.

Perhaps of most interest, al Thani argued that new technology, specifically social media and ubiquitous communications channels, would make it possible to organize these disaffected youth in ways never before experienced in the region. If the Gulf and nearby Arab countries did not wake up to managing their populations' concerns better, he said, governments would be overthrown. Four months later, an uprising that started in Tunisia spread through most of the Arab world, eventually resulting in revolutionary efforts in Bahrain, Egypt, Libya, Syria, and Yemen as well as riots in Algeria, Iran, Iraq, Jordan, Kuwait, Lebanon, Oman, and Sudan. The Egyptian government fell and consequences of the uprising can be seen in the Syrian and Libyan civil wars as well as the extreme violence in Yemen.

When al Thani shared with us his hunches about the region, our group of visiting MBA students was skeptical, believing that the leadership in most of these countries would be able to manage any uprising quite easily. We were wrong, of course; we underestimated the speed with which electronic communications and social media can organize and coordinate activism. As it turned out, the slow machinery of government could not respond quickly enough to dilute the impact of social media. Social media is a powerful tool that can be put in either the right or wrong hands. We would hope that it increasingly serves as the foundation to drive massive, fast *and positive* change. History will ultimately determine whether the Arab Spring was a positive or negative series of events. But what it has told us already about our ability to propel a coordinated effort quickly across national borders is priceless.

◎ ◎ ◎

The fundamental point worth reemphasizing is that we will not be able to address the crises described throughout this book fast enough if we depend on the speed of decision-making and implementation typical of the past seventy years. We need to do some important things on a very big scale, very quickly. Although the world may not be in ruins as it was after World War II, it is at a crucial fork in the road. Our choice of direction could lead to a wonderful life for those who are to follow us, or a world that we will not be proud to bring our children and our grandchildren into. The choice is in our hands and in whether we can revive the ability to achieve massive results quickly.

CHAPTER 12

Leadership:
Reframing Influence

Balancing Paradoxes

Throughout the course of writing this book, we have met some remarkable people. Dynamic and imaginative individuals with uncanny insight who were moved and sufficiently worried by the crises we face to change the trajectory of their regions, institutions, or businesses, preparing them to steer through a difficult and disrupted future and improving the social conditions of the many people dependent on them. By varying degrees, these leaders took the time (or in some cases even made it their life's work) to understand the crises' origins and their threats. And ultimately they provided creative solutions when others were still struggling with identifying the problem. Reflecting on these leaders and why they have been so effective and visionary in the most challenging situations, an unlikely common leadership profile emerges. Each leader reconciled (and used to their advantage) two distinctive characteristics that on the surface seem quite at odds.

Vice Mayor Jin Naibing is steadfastly devoted to Kunshan—where she was born and raised—and yet is globally astute. Marjorie Scardino daringly embraced century-old core traditions at Pearson Plc as the basis of outsized modern innovation. Dennis Snower used remarkable political skills to revive the G20 process, giving it a relevance it had lost, yet somehow maintained a high level of integrity as his primary strength. Jim Danko had the brassy courage to demand that a somewhat sleepy Midwestern university change and modernize quickly and yet relied on deep currents of quiet humility to gain consensus at the school. Microsoft's Satya Nadella has led a company dedicated to software, platforms, and machines and still is a dyed-in-the-wool humanist. And Ravi Venkatesan showed that he is a bold and visionary strategist in designing an organization, the Global Alliance for Mass Entrepreneurship (GAME), that aims to kickstart and train ten million entrepreneurs in India by 2030, yet he also has intense, dynamic, roll-up-your-sleeves executional capabilities.

By deftly integrating opposing traits to fashion a more cohesive, productive, and effective leadership style, these people applied an aspect of what I call the Six Paradoxes of Leadership. In the course of trying to address a complex problem in their context, these leaders learned how to comfortably inhabit both elements of at least one paradox. This is not an easy undertaking. Many leaders—indeed, all of us—gravitate toward our sweet spots; to what we do well. But by definition, leadership paradoxes require that we use our best skills while also improving those traits we would prefer to avoid.

The Six Paradoxes of Leadership work as a system, forcing us to balance competing characteristics, abilities, and beliefs. At the heart of each paradox is a core tension that involves contradictory-yet-interrelated elements that exist simultaneously and persist over time. When these characteristics are out of sync, the outcome is almost always disappointing. Think of the high-profile executive hero who saves an organization from the brink of disaster but lacks the humility to seek advice or the ability to change course; more than likely, that campaign will end in failure.

The six paradoxes explored in this chapter are not the only ones leaders will encounter as they take on the challenges of ADAPT. But I believe they are the most urgent ones for leaders to embrace in today's environment. They represent a fresh approach to leadership utterly necessary for the unique and formidable threats we face and this will likely be true well into the next decade. It probably shouldn't be surprising, considering the contradictions inherent in the crises we are confronting, that these paradoxes have emerged as by-products of a global system that had improved economic and social prospects for millions of people and then suddenly was no longer effective. Great leadership now requires dancing on both sides of a sword.

Paradox 1: Tech-savvy humanist

Competing Capabilities

> *Tech-savvy:* Use and understand technology to drive future success
> *Humanist:* Understand and care about people and organizations and how they function as well as human effectiveness in systems and situations

When you spend some time with Microsoft CEO Satya Nadella, it is striking that in many ways he is a humanist first and a technologist second. He prefers to discuss the purpose of Microsoft and its role in the world and the countries in which it operates and pepper these conversations with comments about technology. Since Nadella became CEO in 2014, Microsoft has consistently been named to numerous "best places to work" lists and he has implemented a new culture at the company that focuses on encouraging employee innovation, breaking down silos and opening doors to communication, offering employees a transparent career path, and linking executive compensation to diversity progress. "If we are going to serve the planet as our mission states, we need to reflect the planet," Nadella has said. To capture his leadership philosophy, he offers this equation:

Empathy + Shared Values + Safety and Reliability = Trust over Time

Of course, Nadella is equally practiced as a technologist. Recently, he has steered Microsoft to new heights in revenue, earnings, and market valuation mostly by remaking the company into a leader in cloud-based networking and software, erasing the memory of the many years that Microsoft floundered around without an Internet strategy. The humanist side of this paradox is a complex quality that includes but also goes far beyond encouraging positive experiences in the workplace. It involves fully understanding how people operate, the impact of systems on them, and how their lives can be augmented rather than diminished by technology. At the same time, it requires caring enough to assess how a technological advance will affect—improve or harm—the people who will be impacted the most by it. This demands an enormous amount of empathy, particularly in predicting the effect of technology that is still on the drawing boards. And it takes a high degree of self-discipline for a technologist to consider and eliminate the negative consequences of technologies they build and put into the marketplace.

It may be tempting to think that having humanists at the top of tech companies will be enough to ensure that these firms are good global citizens, but that is not sufficient. Indeed, the importance of the tech-savvy side of this leadership paradox should not be understated. Technology dominates our lives and affects us in ways previously unseen. Our privacy, livelihoods, quality of life, and social relations are dependent on technology being implemented with care and sensitivity and not malevolently. It is no longer okay to assume technology is benign, nor to hold naïve theories of what technology does to our thinking, emotions, communities, and nations. Only tech-savvy leaders have sufficient technology expertise to build systems that anticipate the future—and thus make sure they are attentive to improving lives, not threatening them. Indeed, leaders fail when they apply technology that solves yesterday's problems and are a detriment to the well-being of individuals and organizations in the years to come. They are not doing their jobs when they lack proper judgment about the consequences of technology or don't take the issue seriously enough.

Paradox 2: High-integrity politician

Competing Capabilities

> *High-integrity:* Maintain integrity and build trust in all interactions
> *Politician:* Accrue support, negotiate, form coalitions, and overcome resistance to create and maintain progress

Dennis Snower, the president of the Global Solutions Initiative whom you met in Chapter 9, took on what could be called an impossible task. And yet he made it possible. To breathe new life into the annual G20 summit— making it worthwhile again as a venue for critical global issues like climate change, resource shortages, and wealth disparity, rather than just host politicians' pet issues—Snower created a framework for continuous agenda building that took into account new and urgent problems and progress made in dealing with past concerns. Putting together this group took remarkable political skills because the range of stakeholders that Snower had to gain agreement from was enormous. He had to make this approach acceptable to political leaders and leading economists and political scientists, all of whom have quite different views on the shape of a new global order. Snower also placed corporate voices into the mix among academics and thinktanks, who are typically highly distrustful of corporations. And he did this in an environment of increasing antagonism and nationalism among many of the G20 countries themselves.

A tough effort, but it was successful only because in the midst of all the political persuasion, negotiation, maneuvering, debate, and deal-making, Snower brought an unwavering sense of purpose, clarity of goal, honesty, and fairness to the process. His political skill produces agreements among many competing interests, but his integrity brings people to the table in the first place and keeps them there. They trust that Snower has everyone's interests at heart and will not lie or mislead just to reach an accord. No one, among the many people involved in this effort, doubted his selflessness or his intentions. How many exceptionally skilled politicians can be described as having an unshakeable sense of integrity and fair play?

Snower's adroit political skills on the base of a foundation of deep integrity serve as a model today as the number and diversity of constituents needed to respond to the issues arising from ADAPT and the four global crises have grown immensely. These issues are increasingly complex and interdependent, which means that solutions depend on corralling a much broader set of stakeholders with a variety of legitimate points of view, diverse considerations, and underlying assumptions. To drive execution in this context, leaders are expected to accrue support, negotiate, form coalitions, anticipate counteractions, and overcome resistance. With more parties at the table, political competence becomes more important than ever before. However, people rarely stay if there is not trust in the process or a mutual belief in the fundamental intentions or that their voice will be valued. To create and sustain such belief requires a high level of integrity.

Often would-be political consensus builders fall short because they forfeit their integrity in deeply political environments. So much time may be spent meeting the needs of everyone and managing the countervailing forces that leaders may sacrifice their core principles for expediency. But precisely because the political landscape today is so polarized and distrustful, only leaders who exhibit transparent integrity and a commitment to the group's goals, rather than individual constituent self-interest, can hope to produce a successful outcome.

Paradox 3: Globally minded localist

Competing Capabilities

- *Globally minded:* Be agnostic about belief system and market structure and be a student of the world

- *Localist:* Have a deep commitment to a place and understand and successfully navigate local market issues and nuances

I introduced you to Jin, vice mayor of Kunshan, in Chapter 4. From our first meeting, it was clear that Jin was deeply devoted to her city and relished showing it off. I was taken to the restaurant that makes the Ao Zao noodles Kunshan is famous for; back in the Qing dynasty an emperor in Beijing sought to steal away the chef who first made these noodles, but the chef, like Jin, loved Kunshan too much to leave. I saw the theater where Chinese opera originated and the art gallery featuring projects from students throughout the city. Jin had me try her favorite local dish, the famous hairy crab fished from the waters of the nearby lakes. She was an unrelenting localist, focused on combining a growth economy with a strong education system and cultural offerings to keep Kunshan thriving.

Jin was also an astute student of the world who saw mounting political fracturing, economic competition, and income disparity well before they were obvious to most of us. She was determined that maintaining Kunshan's success was predicated on attracting Duke University to the city. A world-class school would solidify Kunshan as an innovative region, able to attract students, teachers, researchers, and entrepreneurs from around the world. There would also be increased access to capital and upscale housing and commerce development surrounding the university. In short, she knew that by aligning Duke with Kunshan, the local city would become a global entity.

Jin was prescient in observing that in the early twenty-first century the global worldview was becoming local. People around the world are generally more anxious and concerned about their own and their children's future. In such times, people's focus becomes narrower; they seek others like themselves and turn their attention to issues closer to home. Many of the issues raised through the ADAPT framework are best solved locally. At a national or international level, they seem intractable, or at least opinions are so polarized that it is hard to get agreement.

However, there are momentous challenges that cannot be addressed at a local level: atmosphere, oceans, and pathogens are indifferent to borders. There still remains significant economic interdependence; how we reshape technology to help us be more human is a pan-national issue and there are dramatic disparities across the globe that we should not neglect. This last point is not just a selfless concern. Very poor countries have citizens who emigrate, legally or not, and tend to engage in wars that cross their own borders. We cannot escape each other's problems. Thus it is important for leaders to be able to hold two apparently contradictory mindsets: a local preoccupation with an astute global awareness. Indeed, the ramifications of not embracing both facets of this paradox are palpable. Overemphasis on the global side of the equation results in essentially managing to average— similar to using GDP as a proxy for economic equality across a nation.

On the one hand, it may be obvious that job training is necessary throughout a large region, but individual local areas will have different employment needs and skills; a generalized upskilling program would leave many areas no better off than they were. In fact, it might ignore the places that have the greatest employment needs. On the other hand, die-hard localists without a global vision run the risk of neglecting the fact that we live in a world now built upon interdependence—and while it may be somewhat comforting to believe that local regions can act independent of activities elsewhere, that's a naïve notion. Although local initiatives can drive the growth of local economies, local economies cannot operate on their own. Moreover, global or national economic and social campaigns often have substantial resources to test out a variety of strategic and tactical models, the best of which can be emulated by locally minded innovators.

Paradox 4: Humble hero

Competing Capabilities

> *Humble:* Foster resilience in self and others, recognizing when they need to help and be helped, and demonstrate humility in listening to others

> *Hero:* Make decisions in times of uncertainty and exude confidence with gravitas

Jim Danko, president of Butler University, was highlighted in Chapter 9 for his stunning campaign to move the school forward, out of its inertia, by originating a largely independent arm of the university that could quickly design whole new models of education. In doing this, Danko was courageous enough to ask profound questions about the future of universities and whether it was possible to create the capacity to respond fast enough to the dynamic changes confronting them. These are big, weighty questions, but Danko didn't want to impose his answers on the university. Instead, he listened to responses from the school's board, alumni, students, professors, and other constituents, and he would adopt good ideas he heard even when they opposed his own. In addition, he was willing to admit that he was unsure about his plan, since it was new and untried, and he promised to assess, report back, and fix parts that were broken.

Danko's heroic effort stemmed from the realization that he had to rise up and provide daring leadership to preserve the institution he led. His humility, though, was the reason this effort succeeded. It enabled him to bring the other constituents along, to convince them to collaborate and to have an ongoing plan with university buy-in to assess whether the new initiative needed improvements in the future. His gift was in embracing the humble hero leadership paradox, which can be described best through the question, How do we help leaders to have the fearlessness to act with confidence in an uncertain world and the humility to recognize when they are wrong or haven't asked the right questions to get the optimal answers?

Given the number of fast-changing variables that leaders face today, taking action becomes incredibly difficult. The tough challenge is for the leader to provide clarity in the moments when, even for them, things are least clear. Yet, more than ever, leaders feel as if they need to behave like heroes, exuding self-assurance in anxiety-inducing times. That's okay as long as they don't combine this heroism with the arrogance to presume that they know all the answers and to be unwilling to change course when insurmountable challenges arise or others in their orbit offer helpful suggestions. The speed and enormity of change today requires leaders who can decide and act with alacrity but also have the humility to recognize the limits of their abilities and the courage to admit their mistakes.

But there is another aspect to being humble that is equally important: inclusivity. True leaders can avoid mistakes by encouraging input from all the people who will be impacted by a decision or who have a great deal of expertise to offer. By seeking opinions, background materials, data, and anecdotal evidence from a large and diverse contingent of people, leaders allow everyone to feel like they had in a hand in the final decision and hence, choices that turn out to be mistakes can be quickly rectified as a team effort. Of course, sometimes too much varied input can paralyze leaders, who become afraid to make a decision because they are presented with an array of complex and nuanced pieces of solutions to a problem. That's when the heroic aspect of this leadership paradox must kick in. By not making any decision, a leader is actually making a decision to do nothing and the organization or region will fall behind in today's dynamic landscape. Real leaders would have the courage to make a decision based on what they know and be ready to change course if the chosen option turns out to be in error.

It takes profound personal resilience for leaders to admit when they are wrong, allow others to make mistakes, be inclusive in seeking advice, make hard decisions based on what their gut tells them, and foster confidence to stimulate ongoing success. It demonstrates vulnerability and in the process leaders become more human to their colleagues. In turn, these paradoxical elements of the humble hero serve as a springboard for facing the future.

Paradox 5: Traditioned innovator

Competing Capabilities

> *Traditioned:* Connect deeply with the purpose of the organization or place—especially the original ideas that served as its foundation—and bring these values to the present day

> *Innovator:* Drive innovation, try new things, and have the courage to
> fail and allow others to do so

Marjorie Scardino, CEO of Pearson Plc, who appears in chapter 9, recognized that the strength of her company was in its traditions. Rich, smart,
accurate, and credible journalism are the bread and butter of Pearson's *Financial Times* and the *Economist* (in which Pearson owns a 50 percent stake).
The company's educational offerings were also well respected and deeply entrenched in the organization's DNA. Less so was an array of other businesses
in technology, investment banking, and waxworks. Scardino's challenge was
to maintain the company's traditional strengths, protecting its essential character while developing new channels and updated products that would allow
the company to survive the technology disruption facing old media. Many
other brand-name media outfits—Time Inc. is an obvious example—were
unable to make the transition that Scardino handled so nimbly.

To describe leaders like Scardino, I coined the term traditioned innovator—someone who respects the traditions of the institutions they are
leading but realizes that to preserve what is significant about those institutions you need meaningful innovation. This phrase first came to mind in
a conversation with my closest colleague at Duke University, Greg Jones,
the dean of the Divinity School where clergy are trained. He described the
challenges of changing a school so deeply founded on tradition, one where
a single very old text served as the basis for all of its research and teaching.
Jones saw the need for greater integration with other schools, research and
teaching focused on the increasingly multidisciplinary problems of the day,
the changes needed to develop religious leaders in an increasingly secular
society, and the need to recast ideas such as character and virtue in today's
world. I made the irreverent observation that his problem boiled down to
a simple question: How do you tell your faculty, board members, alumni,
allied churches, and students that God was wrong ten years ago? We determined that a better way to put it was, How do you translate the traditions
and truths of the past in a manner still relevant to these times?

It was essential for Scardino to hold on to the products that Pearson was best known for and the best historical qualities that Pearson possessed because these gave Pearson value. These traditions are precisely what is needed in the ADAPT environment—media that is fair, neutral, and covers the world from a sophisticated perch. At the same time, innovation is non-negotiable. All organizations need to transform, not just once but often as global gears shift. Leaders must ensure that transformation occurs by creating a culture that will drive their organization into new areas, technologies, methods, products, and services, and (perhaps most important) new ideas, since relying on outmoded ways of thinking without questioning or updating them has been the prime contributor to institutional irrelevance today.

But instead of traditioned innovation, would it make more sense to just break the organization and move on? Split the paradox and throw out the traditioned part? For most institutions that is a foolhardy approach. After all, the value of what institutions like the media, government, education, markets, policing, and defense have provided is not in question—it is just as important now as it was in the past. The inability of these institutions to change and modernize is the critical shortcoming. Some media companies have in fact attempted to ride out the disruption in their sector by, for instance, adulterating the journalism they were known for. They chase Internet clicks with poorly written, unsourced, sensationalist articles instead of trying to serve the better angels of their readers. Many of those media outfits have not survived, enmeshed in a digital revenue squeeze as they and hundreds of others on the Web race to the bottom.

By respecting tradition, leaders are more apt to adopt appropriate and more impactful innovation because they took the time to understand the core purpose of their organization—and to carry that purpose forward into a more modern manifestation. That, in turn, gives the evolving organization a foundation to build upon. The traditioned innovator paradox can best be summarized by the somewhat Confucian suggestion that leaders remember that they are hosts to those who came before, who are sitting on their shoulders watching what they are doing, reminding them how they got here and urging them not to destroy the organization's legacy through inaction.

Paradox 6: Strategic executor

Competing Capabilities

> *Strategic:* Use insights about the future to inform today's decision making

> *Executor:* Deliver exquisitely on today's challenges

As someone who is responsible for the strategy of a large organization, I find this last paradox a bit humbling. The global landscape is changing far too quickly for me to have the luxury to sit back, review what's going on, debate it at length, and come up with a grand scheme to be reviewed and implemented some five years later. Not anymore. Yet there are extremely long-term trends and intermediate-term issues that we need to prepare for as we respond to the immediate pressures and significant short-term issues. The answer is to not separate execution from strategy. We need to execute with the future in mind, or strategize while executing.

Ravi Venkatesan, the founder of GAME, exemplifies the strategic executor paradox. On the one hand, he is the consummate big-firm strategist able to put a grand vision and a large organization together in a manner that reveals expertise picked up during decades of work in the corporate world. (He was chairman of the Bank of Baroda, India's second largest bank, and before that, chairman of Microsoft India). On the other hand, Venkatesan is dedicated to creating local opportunities for a large number of entrepreneurs through GAME, an effort that will epitomize learning and adjusting rapidly to changing conditions in the start-up sphere.

His organizational framework has two distinct elements: (1) an overall architecture and governance structure that will be relatively permanent and hew to principles that Venkatesan designed, based on experience, to facilitate GAME's mandate; and (2) a dynamic operational model that will be in flux; constantly improving as new ideas emerge. In the first part, Venkatesan demonstrates the execution aspect of the strategic executor paradox; in the second, he provides the strategic dimension. Perhaps the most impressive element of his approach to GAME is that without the disciplined structure and the concomitant rules and policies that he put in place—without the exquisitely drawn execution game plan for governance and growth—the organization would be adrift and unable to meet the goals of its strategic thrust.

When execution and strategy are not in balance, success is anything but certain. Leaders who favor execution over strategy are setting themselves up for failure because they could be caught in the vicious cycle of constantly fixing problems within systems but not addressing flaws in the system itself. On the one hand, they go from fix to fix without making material progress—progress that would be possible if there was a strategic plan for how the system is expected to serve the organization's goals in the coming years. Moreover, these execution-heavy leaders are trapped, focusing on today's problems rather than what the future requires. Dynamic innovation is at a premium when a leader approaches developing a system or an organizational plan in this way.

On the other hand, a leader who is "all strategy, no execution" won't remain in the job very long because the organization will lack the capacity to actually address issues that must be tackled for its survival. If you can't fix the small things in front of you, you will certainly be unable to solve the larger problems that are yet to materialize. Most organizations will oust the leader who is ill-equipped to deal with obvious day-to-day dilemmas. Also, systems, structures, or programs that are not executed well will chew up resources—financial, workforce, political—in the short-term and leave nothing for the longer horizon. People usually have an inclination toward strategy or execution. To overcome that, a leader should articulate a strategy but with a clear understanding that it probably needs to evolve and execute with both immediate needs and the changing future in mind.

◎ ◎ ◎

For people in roles like mine, present success and future vision executed brilliantly and together are essential today. It seems daunting perhaps to effectively reconcile all Six Paradoxes of Leadership, which is why good leaders know what their strengths are—and the leadership paradox they are most suited to navigate. They must develop complementary leaders around them who are more comfortable managing through other paradoxes. In exploring these leadership paradoxes and the remarkable people who have excelled, I am struck by how deeply each leader cares about the leadership tasks they have before them. They care enough to face very large questions affecting the future of their towns, organizations, businesses, and institutions with both courage and depth, to understand what is at the heart of the challenges and what it will take to find a way to overcome them. I can't help but think that if we all cared more about finding solutions and building bridges of trust that welcome the input of people around us, the leadership paradoxes would not seem quite so difficult to resolve.

A Note on COVID-19

In the time between submitting the manuscript to the publisher and finalizing the editing process for this book, the world has been consumed by the coronavirus. The challenges this pandemic presents are accelerating the crises we identified in these pages. The extreme but necessary measures taken by nations around the world to flatten the infection curve will have major impacts on the global economy, and those in the most fragile groups will suffer increasing asymmetry. Technology offers us some big advantages in combating the virus, but social media is fragmenting and multiplying messages, creating confusion and sometimes panic. The challenges aging populations pose to inadequate healthcare systems have been fast-forwarded and are now at the heart of the crisis. Polarization and the general lack of trust make it difficult for societies to act in concert when it is most crucial to do so.

Yet the solutions presented in these pages offer hope at a time when it is so desperately needed. The lack of local resources and the need to localize some manufacturing is evident from critical shortages experienced during the pandemic, but institutions are rapidly acknowledging the need to get significantly better at doing massive things quickly and well. Indeed, some of the most impressive and strongest responses are coming from communities. Scientific and pharmaceutical industries are moving to a wartime footing to scale up solutions. And, paradoxically, the extreme nature of social isolation is bringing people together through virtual means as they share their common experiences.

The coronavirus pandemic is clearly a watershed event for humanity. The question is, will we take the best from our responses to the challenge and apply it to the crises outlined in this book, or will we expend all our energy on solving the short-term problem and put longer-horizon issues on the back burner? We have a chance to remake the world on better terms and take decisions now that will bring us out of COVID-19 stronger, with lessons learned, and in a way that prepares us for the future. If we don't choose that path, we will prolong the suffering, and midnight may come even sooner. If we build on the emerging sense of cooperation and focus on the common good and what is important in life, dawn may come even sooner that we could have hoped.

Epilogue

This book is about the worries our team heard and translated into the ADAPT framework; the crises that result from those worries that will produce irreversible consequences across the world if we don't act now; and the argument for why we have a mere ten years to midnight with the clock ticking. Yet I believe there is reason not to despair. Many times in our history we have seen that when a common enemy emerges, people come together in significant collaboration to restore balance. We are at such a point now. I hope that readers realize I see our future through an optimistic lens.

At the same time, the need to rethink our course has never been more obvious—or more urgent. Everyone should participate in this. Every step taken by each individual is precious and should be taken with intention, from the small and individual constructive actions we all can embrace by adjusting our daily lives, changing our behaviors, and building new and more responsible habits, to the *massive, fast* solutions leaders should be chasing that could positively influence and improve the lives of thousands or millions of people. No one is exempt from the need to act. Please decide what role you will play and get to it.

NOTES

PART I: HOW WE GOT TO THE PRECIPICE

1. These ideas were first developed jointly with my colleague Colm Kelly; see Colm Kelly and Blair Sheppard, "Common Purpose: Realigning Business, Economics, and Society," *Strategy + Business*, May 25, 2017, https://www.strategy -business.com/author?author=Colm+Kelly. Kelly focuses on how we rethink economics and better link social good to economic success; see Kelly and Sheppard, "Creating Common Purpose," PwC, 2018, https://www.pwc.com/gx/en/issues /assets/pdf/pwc-creating-common-purpose-2018-global-solutions.pdf (accessed February 4, 2020).

Chapter 1
What Worries Us

1. "Amit Chandra Becomes a Voice for Philanthropy," The Bridgespan Group, October 11, 2016, https://www.bridgespan.org/insights/library/remarkable-givers /profiles/amit-chandra-voice-for-philanthropy.

2. For a summary of this work, see Blair Sheppard and Ceri-Ann Droog, "A Crisis of Legitimacy," *Strategy + Business*, June 5, 2019, https://www.strategy-business.com /article/A-crisis-of-legitimacy.

3. UBS and PwC, *Billionaires Insights 2018*.

4. OECD, *The Squeezed Middle Class in OECD and Emerging Countries: Myth and Reality*, December 2016.

5. International Labour Organization, *Global Wage Report*, various years.

6. Alicia Hall, "Trends in Home Ownership in Australia: A Quick Guide," Parliament of Australia, June 28, 2017, https://www.aph.gov.au/About_Parliament /Parliamentary_Departments/Parliamentary_Library/pubs/rp/rp1617/Quick _Guides/TrendsHomeOwnership.

7. Elisa Shearer, "Social Media Outpaces Print Newspapers in the US as a News Source," Pew Research, December 10, 2018, https://www.pewresearch.org/fact-tank /2018/12/10/social-media-outpaces-print-newspapers-in-the-u-s-as-a-news-source/.

8. Oliver Milman, "Defiant Mark Zuckerberg Defends Facebook Policy to Allow False Ads," *The Guardian*, December 2, 2019, https://www.theguardian.com /technology/2019/dec/02/mark-zuckerberg-facebook-policy-fake-ads.

9. David Marquand, "The People Is Sublime: The Long History of Populism, from Robespierre to Trump," *The New Statesman*, July 24, 2017.

Chapter 2
Assymetry and the Crisis of Prosperity

1. Francis Fukuyama, *The End of History and the Last Man* (New York: Free Press, 1992).

2. "Hamilton Population," World Population Review, http://worldpopulation review.com/world-cities/hamilton-population/ (accessed February 21, 2020).

3. For example, Hamilton was chosen as one of twenty-one smart cities by the Intelligent Community Forum. See Rodney Barnes, "Hamilton among the ICF's Smart21 Communities of 2020," October 27, 2019, https://softwarehamilton.com /2019/10/27/hamilton-among-the-icfs-smart21-communities-of-2020/. Bob Young, the founder of Red Hat and Lulu, hails from Hamilton.

4. "A Brief History of Ontarion Wine," Niagara Vintage Wine Tours blog, https://www.niagaravintagewinetours.com/a-brief-history-of-ontarion-wine/ (accessed February 21, 2020).

5. "Property Prices in Berlin," Numbeo, https://www.numbeo.com/property -investment/in/Berlin (accessed February 21, 2020).

6. "Moscow Real Estate Prices among World's Fastest-Growing," *Moscow Times*, April 12, 2019.

7. "Two-thirds of U.K. Students Will Never Pay Off Debt," *Financial Times*, July 4, 2016.

8. "America Can Fix Its Student Loan Crisis. Just Ask Australia," *New York Times*, July 9, 2016.

9. "Pension Participation of All Workers by Type of Plan, 1989–2016," Center for Retirement Research at Boston College, http://crr.bc.edu/wp-content/uploads /2015/10/Pension-coverage.pdf (accessed February 21, 2020).

10. GOBankingRanks survey 2018, updated on September 23, 2019, https://www .gobankingrates.com/retirement/planning/why-americans-will-retire-broke/.

11. "Russia Population 2020," *World Population Review*, http://worldpopulation review.com/countries/russia-population/ (accessed February 21, 2020).

12. "China's AI Push Raises Fears over Widespread Job Cuts," *Financial Times*, August 30, 2018.

Chapter 3
Disruption and the Crisis of Technology

1. For a good and entertaining discussion of massive disruptions in history, see Dan Carlin, *The End Is Always Near: Apocalyptic Moments, from the Bronze Age Collapse to Nuclear Near Misses* (New York: HarperCollins, 2019).

2. One interesting example is the ongoing debate between Elon Musk and Bill Gates about the risks of artificial intelligence. See "Bill Gates: I Do Not Agree with Elon Musk about AI," CNBC, September 25, 2017, https://www.cnbc.com/2017/09/25/bill-gates-disagrees-with-elon-musk-we-shouldnt-panic-about-a-i.html.

3. Two fairly engaging treatments of the predominance of a few platform companies and their larger consequences are Scott Galloway, *The Four: The Hidden DNA of Amazon, Apple, Facebook, and Google* (New York: Portfolio/Penguin, 2017); and Martin Moore and Damian Tambini, *Digital Dominance: The Power of Google, Amazon, Facebook and Apple* (New York: Oxford University Press, 2018).

4. See Robert H. Frank and Phil J. Cook, *Winner Take All Society: Why the Few at the Top Get So Much More Than the Rest of Us* (New York: Penguin Books, 1995).

5. For a recent summary of this idea, see Philip Cooke, *Knowledge Economies: Clusters, Leaning and Cooperative Advantage* (London: Routledge, 2002).

6. "States of Growth: Gujarat, Madhya Pradesh, Haryana, Fastest-Growing Punjab, Uttar Pradesh, Kerala Bring Up the Rear," CRISIL, January 2018, https://www.crisil.com/content/dam/crisil/our-analysis/reports/Research/documents/2017/CRISIL-Research-Insight-States-of-growth.pdf.

7. Richard Edelman, quoted in "Upskilling: Bridging the Digital Divide," PwC, December 1, 2019, https://www.youtube.com/watch?v=8HE43CFLiag&feature=youtu.be&list=PLnF8iaZwgjXnfrw-iTrzax7voupMisodt.

8. C. Frey and M. Osborne, "The Future of Employment: How Susceptible Are Jobs to Computerisation," Oxford Martin School, University of Oxford, 2013.

9. "How Will Automation Impact Jobs?," PwC, https://www.pwc.co.uk/services/economics-policy/insights/the-impact-of-automation-on-jobs.html (accessed February 20, 2020).

10. Frey's book is a comprehensive and compelling look at the intermediate consequences of the Industrial Revolution and its implications for the world we are entering. See Carl Benedikt Frey, *The Technology Trap: Capital, Labor, and Power in the Age of Automation* (Princeton, NJ: Princeton University Press, 2019).

11. D. Zissis and D. Lekkas, "Addressing Cloud Computing Security Issues," *Future Generation Computing Systems* 28, no. 3 (March 2012): 583–92.

12. "Big Brother Is Watching: How China Is Compiling Computer Ratings on ALL Its Citizens," *South China Morning Post*, November 24, 2015, https://www.scmp.com/news/china/policies-politics/article/1882533/big-brother-watching-how-china-compiling-computer.

13. For a good general discussion of why people are more preoccupied with bad than good, see Roy F. Baumeister, Ellen Bratslavsky, Catrin Finkenauer, et al., "Bad Is Stronger Than Good," *Sage Journals*, December 1, 2001, https://journals.sagepub.com /doi/abs/10.1037/1089-2680.5.4.323.

14. Mike Allen, "Sean Parker Unloads on Facebook," *Axios*, November 9, 2017, https://www.axios.com/sean-parker-unloads-on-facebook-god-only-knows-what-its -doing-to-our-childrens-brains-1513306792-f855e7b4-4e99-4d60-8d51-2775559c2671 .html.

15. Adam Gazzaley and Larry Rosen, *The Distracted Mind: Ancient Brains in a High-Tech World* (Cambridge, MA: MIT Press, 2016), 115.

16. Gazzaley and Rosen, *Distracted Mind*, 116.

17. "About Max Tegmark," Future of Life Institute, https://futureoflife.org /author/max/ (accessed February 20, 2020).

Chapter 4
Trust and the Crisis of Institutional Legitimacy

1. Samuel P. Huntington, *The Clash of Civilizations and the Remaking of the World Order* (New York: Simon & Schuster, 1996).

2. "Fourth Estate," https://en.wikipedia.org/wiki/Fourth_Estate (accessed February 20, 2020).

3. Pew Research, "Trusting the News Media in the Trump Era," surveys conducted between November 27 and December 10, 2018, and February 19 and March 2, 2019, https://www.journalism.org/2019/12/12/highly-engaged-partisans -have-starkly-different-views-of-the-news-media/.

4. "Media Companies Dominate Most Divisive Brands List, and It Keeps Getting Worse," *Morning Consult*, October 1, 2019, https://morningconsult.com/2019 /10/01/polarizing-brands-2019/.

5. Amy Mitchell, Jeffrey Gottfried, Jocelyn Kiley, and Katerina Eva Matsa, "Political Polarization and Media Habits," Pew Research Center, October 21, 2014, https://www.journalism.org/2014/10/21/political-polarization-media-habits/.

6. Justin McCurry, "Trade Wars, Tweets, and Western Liberalism: G20 Summit Wraps Up in Osaka," *Guardian*, June 29, 2019, https://www.theguardian.com/world /2019/jun/29/g20-summit-osaka-japan-trade-wars-liberalism.

7. John Gerald Ruggie, *Multilateralism Matters: The Theory and Praxis of Institutional Form* (New York: Columbia University Press, 1993).

8. Chichun Fang, "Growing Wealth Gaps in Education," Institute for Social Research, University of Michigan, June 20, 2018, https://www.src.isr.umich.edu/blog /growing-wealth-gaps-in-education/; and D. D. Guttenplan, "Measuring the Wealth Effect in Education," *New York Times*, December 2, 2013, https://www.nytimes.com /2013/12/02/world/europe/measuring-the-wealth-effect-in-education.html.

9. *Revenue Stats 2019: Tax Revenue Trends in the OECD*, OECD, https://www
.oecd.org/tax/tax-policy/revenue-statistics-highlights-brochure.pdf (accessed
February 20, 2020).

Chapter 5
Polarization and the Crisis of Leadership

1. "Species and Climate Change," IUCN, https://www.iucn.org/theme/species
/our-work/species-and-climate-change (accessed February 21, 2020); "Climate
Change," Great Barrier Reef Foundation, https://www.barrierreef.org/the-reef
/the-threats/climate-change (accessed February 20, 2020); Scott A. Kulp and
Benjamin H. Strauss, "New Elevation Data Triple Estimates of Global Vulnerability
to Sea-Level Rise and Coastal Flooding," *Nature Communications*, 2019, https://
doi.org/10.1038/s41467-019-12808-7; and Ellen Gray and Jessica Merzdorf, "Earth's
Freshwater Future: Extremes of Flood and Drought," NASA, June 13, 2019, https://
www.nasa.gov/feature/goddard/2019/earth-s-freshwater-future-extremes-of-flood
-and-drought.

2. Ellen Gray, "Unexpected Future Boost of Methane Possible from Arctic
Permafrost," NASA, August 20, 2018, https://climate.nasa.gov/news/2785
/unexpected-future-boost-of-methane-possible-from-arctic-permafrost/.

3. Erik C. Nisbet, Kathryn E. Cooper, and R. Kelly Garrett, "The Partisan Brain:
How Dissonant Science Messages Lead Conservatives and Liberals to (Dis)Trust
Science," *American Academy of Political and Social Science*, February 8, 2015.

4. Greg Lukianoff and Jonathan Haidt, "The Coddling of the American Mind,"
The Atlantic (September 2015), https://www.theatlantic.com/magazine/archive
/2015/09/the-coddling-of-the-american-mind/399356/.

5. "Climate Action Tracker," https://climateactiontracker.org/countries/
(accessed February 20, 2020).

6. William Forster Lloyd, "Two Lectures on the Checks to Population," 1833.

Chapter 6
Age, Accelerating the Four Crises

1. "Japan's Glut of Abandoned Homes: Hard To Sell but Bargains When
Opportunity Knocks," *Japan Times*, December 26, 2017.

2. "Japan's Glut of Abandoned Homes."

3. *The World Factbook*, CIA, https://www.cia.gov/library/publications/
resources/the-world-factbook/fields/343rank.html (accessed February 20, 2020).

4. *The World Factbook 2020* (Washington, DC: Central Intelligence Agency,
2020), https://www.cia.gov/library/publications/resources/the-world-factbook
/index.html./

5. "Future of India: The Winning Leap," PwC, https://www.pwc.com/sg/en
/publications/assets/future-of-india-the-winning-leap.pdf (accessed February 20,
2020).

6. Council on Foreign Relations, "The State of US Infrastructure," January 12, 2018.

7. OECD Health Statistics, 2018; PwC analysis.

PART II: CONQUERING THE CRISES

Chapter 7
Strategy: Rethinking Economic Growth—Local First

1. Colm Kelly and Blair Sheppard, "Common Purpose Realigning Business Economies and Societies," *Strategy + Business*, May 25, 2017, https://www.strategy-business.com/feature/Common-Purpose-Realigning-Business-Economies-and-Society?gko=d465f.

2. Kelly and Sheppard, "Common Purpose Realigning Business Economies and Societies."

3. "Tatev Revival," IDeA Foundation, https://www.idea.am/tatev-revival-project (accessed February 20, 2020).

4. "Aurora Humanitarian Initiative," IDeA Foundation, https://www.idea.am/aurora (accessed February 20, 2020).

Chapter 8
Strategy: Reimagining Success—Thriving in a Broken World

1. PwC, "22nd Annual Global CEO Survey," 2019, https://www.pwc.com/gx/en/ceo-survey/2019/report/pwc-22nd-annual-global-ceo-survey.pdf (accessed March 9, 2019).

2. T. Plate, *Conversations with Lee Kuan Yew, Citizen Singapore: How To Build a Nation* (Singapore: Marshall Cavendish, 2010), 46–47.

3. Stuart Anderson, "International Students Are Founding America's Great Startups," *Forbes,* Nov. 5, 2018; www.forbes.com/sites/stuartanderson/2018/11/05/international-students-are-founding-americas-great-startups/#754059e65568

Chapter 9
Structure: Repairing Failing Institutions—Cementing the Foundations

1. A full-blown discussion of institutions and debates about them would take a book. For those who are interested, you might begin with Vivien Lowndes and Mark Roberts, *Why Institutions Matter: The New Institutionalism in Political Science* (London: Red Globe Press, 2013).

2. As a starting point for a review of change management, it is worth going to the person I consider the greatest authority: John P. Kotter, *Leading Change* (Boston: Harvard Business Press, 2012).

3. "Prof. Dennis J. Snower, Ph.D.," Global Solutions: World Policy Forum, https://www.global-solutions.international/cv-snower (accessed February 20, 2020).

4. Dennis Snower, "G20 Summit Was More Successful Than You Think," *G20 Insights*, July 11, 2017, https://www.g20-insights.org/2017/07/11/g20-summit -successful-think/.

5. It was through this process that I first got to know Dennis. He heard of the work my colleague Colm Kelly and I were engaged in and sought our input on the creation of the initial narrative and the design and ongoing operation of the Global Solutions Summit. The core ideas of our work are captured in Kelly and Sheppard, "Common Purpose: Realigning Business, Economies, and Society," *Strategy + Business*, May 25, 2017, https://www.strategy-business.com/feature/Common -Purpose-Realigning-Business-Economies-and-Society?gko=d465f.

6. "President Dennis J. Snower's Opening Address at the Global Solutions Initiative," June 5, 2019, https://www.youtube.com/watch?v=c8sstzOUYtg.

7. C. Stewart Gillmor, *Fred Terman at Stanford: Building a Discipline, a University, and Silicon Valley* (Palo Alto, CA: Stanford University Press, 2004).

Chapter 10
Culture: Refreshing Technology—Innovation as a Social Good

1. Pew Research, "Automation in Everyday Life," survey conducted between May 1 and 15, 2017, https://www.pewresearch.org/internet/2017/10/04/americans -attitudes-toward-a-future-in-which-robots-and-computers-can-do-many-human -jobs/.

2. Satya Nadella, Greg Shaw, and Jill Tracie Nichols, *Hit Refresh: The Quest To Rediscover Microsoft's Soul and Imagine a Better Future for Everyone* (San Francisco: HarperCollins, 2017).

3. George Gilder, *Life after Google: The Fall of Big Data and the Rise of the Blockchain Economy* (Latham, MD: Regnery Gateway, 2018).

4. "What Is Responsible AI," PwC, https://www.pwc.com/gx/en/issues/data -and-analytics/artificial-intelligence/what-is-responsible-ai/responsible-ai-practical -guide.pdf (accessed February 20, 2020).

5. World Health Organization, *Depression and Other Common Mental Disorders: Global Health Estimates* (Geneva: WHO, 2017).

6. Alison Abbott, "Gaming Improves Multitasking Skills," *Nature*, September 4, 2013, https://www.nature.com/news/gaming-improves-multitasking-skills-1.13674.

Chapter 11
Massive and Fast—Problems That Cannot Wait

1. Intergovernmental Panel on Climate Change, https://www.ipcc.ch (accessed February 20, 2020).

2. Glenn Hubbard and William Duggan, "The Forgotten Lessons of the Marshall Plan," *Strategy + Business* (Summer 2008), https://www.strategy-business.com /article/08203?gko=4209e.

3. Global Alliance for Mass Entrepreneurship, https://massentrepreneurship.org (accessed February 20, 2020).

4. Kenichi Ohmae, "The Rise of the Region State," *Foreign Affairs*, March 1, 1993, https://www.foreignaffairs.com/articles/1993-03-01/rise-region-state.

5. Smart Africa, https://smartafrica.org (accessed February 20, 2020).

6. John M. Logsdon, "John F. Kennedy's Space Legacy and Its Lessons for Today," *Issues in Science and Technology* 27 (3): 29–34.

7. "Twenty Things We Wouldn't Have without Space Travel" (infographic), Jet Propulsion Laboratory California Institute of Technology, https://www.jpl.nasa.gov /infographics/infographic.view.php?id=11358 (accessed February 20, 2020).

8. Paul Hawken, *Drawdown: The Most Comprehensive Plan Ever Proposed to Reverse Global Warming* (New York: Penguin Books, 2017).

ACKNOWLEDGMENTS

Writing this book has been one of the highlights of a professional life that I have felt lucky to lead. Not only has it forced me to put into words with some degree of permanence the system of thinking that has formed my worldview for a number of years, and test it against the real challenges we face today, the experience has also enabled me to work deeply with some people I really admire. To my team—Susannah, Ceri-Ann, Alexis, Tom, and Daria—I am proud to have your names alongside mine on the cover of this book that represents the core ideas of our work over the past five years. Thank you for co-creating, researching, writing, and debating with me, and let's keep doing it even now the book is finished. A sincere thank-you to your loved ones whom you don't see enough because of the work you do, but for whom you do everything: Mike, Jess, Katie, and William; Adam, Mia, and Josh; Daniel, Beatrix, and Gus; Katy, Geoff, and Sharyl; Natalia Viktorovna and Nikolay Ivanovich. And to Jeff—thank you for joining the team and helping to ensure our thoughts and ideas were written in a way that will hopefully connect to our readers and inspire the action we need.

The people from around the world at PwC who supported us in creating this book are almost too many to name, but some absolutely must be. Colm Kelly was a formidable thought partner; Kevin Ellis caused us to create the first version of the strategy for the UK by inviting me to speak with his partners and supporting the publication of this book; and Bob Moritz championed these ideas and is staking the future of the PwC Network on solving some of these challenges. Smart and committed partners and staff from a number of countries tested ADAPT and its implications in their local markets and challenged us to develop our thinking. Particular thanks are due to Yoshiaki Matsuda, Michael Ey, and Tidyan Bah as well as people from our firms in Australia, Brazil, Canada, China, Germany, Hungary, India, Italy, Japan, Mexico, the Middle East, Russia, Spain, South Africa, the UK, and the United States. Jenny Forrest, along with Steve Harkin and Delanie Carney, designed a beautiful book cover. Susan Ellis moved mountains for us and made it look easy. Andrea Feeley was the first person to read the book outside the writing team and offered research and insight to help us tell our story. Art Kleiner gave time and energy he did not have to make the book better. Gretchen Anderson introduced us to our publisher, Berrett-Koehler.

I had not known how perfect a fit Berrett-Koehler would be for this book until we met the team in December 2019. We owe a great debt to Neal Maillet, Michael Crowley, and Valerie Caldwell, as well as David Peattie of BookMatters in particular for shepherding this book through the complex business of publication. We also owe a debt to our amazing copyeditor, Amy Smith Bell, who not only understood what we were trying to say but helped us to say it so much better. I want to extend sincere thanks to Steve Piersanti for establishing a publishing house that cares about curating books that challenge and inspire but also offer sustainable solutions for a future in which we all want to live. I am proud to be collaborating with you.

There are a few people whose opinions I have trusted for many years, who have never yet given me bad advice. They have made my ideas better and my experience of the world brighter: Greg Jones, Roy Lewicki, Tony O'Driscoll, Richard Oldfield, Alan Schwartz, Megan Overbay, Jaivir Singh, and Luke Hanguo Li. But no one has done this more than my wife, Martha. She has heard every idea I've ever had, advised me which to pursue and which to drop, and supported her infuriating spouse for more than thirty years. She also gave me our sons, Phil and Chris, who in turn have brought us Lorie, Ellery, and Leighton. Without their patience, challenge, and sticky fingers, it would be harder to remain an optimist and to have the energy to keep trying to build a better future.

INDEX

Page numbers with *f* refer to figures, *t* refer to tables, and *n* refers to notes.

ABOUT THE AUTHORS

JAMES NUBILE

Blair H. Sheppard joined PwC in June 2012 as global leader, strategy and leadership. Before that, he spent the majority of his career as a professor and leader at the Fuqua School of Business, Duke University. During his tenure, in addition to his teaching and research activities, Sheppard was associate dean for executive education, senior associate dean, and dean. He was also the founding CEO and chairman of Duke Corporate Education, rated by leading business journals as the world's top provider of custom executive education during and following his tenure. Sheppard was the primary architect of Duke Kunshan University, Duke's campus in China, which opened in 2014. He is also a proud husband, father, and grandfather.

Five of the authors are members of Sheppard's team at PwC—each of them a director in global strategy and leadership.

Susannah Anfield has worked for PwC and its legacy firms since 1994 and has extensive experience in leadership and senior talent development as well as being an executive coach in systems psychodynamic coaching, accredited with Tavistock, UK. In addition, she is a chartered accountant,

(left to right) **Daria Zarubina, Alexis Jenkins, Thomas Minet, Ceri-Ann Droog, Susannah Anfield, and Jeffrey Rothfeder**

ICAEW, and holds a bachelor's of science in geography from Birmingham University.

Ceri-Ann Droog has worked for PwC since 2008. Previous roles include UK board strategy and serving clients on deals strategy. Before joining PwC, Droog was a business strategy manager at Ford Motor Company for eight years. She is an Oxford engineering and Cranfield MBA graduate.

Alexis Jenkins has worked for PwC since 2013 across the domains of strategy, leadership, and culture and is chief of staff for the team. Before this, Jenkins was regional director for Europe at Duke University's Fuqua School of Business. She studied English, drama, and education at the University of Cambridge.

Thomas Minet has worked for PwC and its legacy firms since 1984. He has specialized in the areas of strategic and scenario planning, large account management, business development, market analysis, and competitive intelligence.

Daria Zarubina has worked for PwC since 2016 in both the Middle East and Russia firms. Previously Zarubina served as regional director for Russia and CIS at Duke University's Fuqua School of Business. She holds an engineering degree from Saint Petersburg State University of Airspace Instrumentation (SUAI) and a management degree from Saint Petersburg State as well as an MBA from the University of Cambridge.

Jeffrey Rothfeder has written about business and technology for the *New Yorker*, the *New York Times*, *Business Week*, *Strategy + Business*, and numerous other publications. He is the author of eight books, including *Driving Honda* (Portfolio) and *Privacy for Sale* (Simon & Schuster).

Berrett–Koehler
Publishers

Berrett-Koehler is an independent publisher dedicated to an ambitious mission: *Connecting people and ideas to create a world that works for all.*

Our publications span many formats, including print, digital, audio, and video. We also offer online resources, training, and gatherings. And we will continue expanding our products and services to advance our mission.

We believe that the solutions to the world's problems will come from all of us, working at all levels: in our society, in our organizations, and in our own lives. Our publications and resources offer pathways to creating a more just, equitable, and sustainable society. They help people make their organizations more humane, democratic, diverse, and effective (and we don't think there's any contradiction there). And they guide people in creating positive change in their own lives and aligning their personal practices with their aspirations for a better world.

And we strive to practice what we preach through what we call "The BK Way." At the core of this approach is *stewardship,* a deep sense of responsibility to administer the company for the benefit of all of our stakeholder groups, including authors, customers, employees, investors, service providers, sales partners, and the communities and environment around us. Everything we do is built around stewardship and our other core values of *quality, partnership, inclusion,* and *sustainability.*

This is why Berrett-Koehler is the first book publishing company to be both a B Corporation (a rigorous certification) and a benefit corporation (a for-profit legal status), which together require us to adhere to the highest standards for corporate, social, and environmental performance. And it is why we have instituted many pioneering practices (which you can learn about at www.bkconnection.com), including the Berrett-Koehler Constitution, the Bill of Rights and Responsibilities for BK Authors, and our unique Author Days.

We are grateful to our readers, authors, and other friends who are supporting our mission. We ask you to share with us examples of how BK publications and resources are making a difference in your lives, organizations, and communities at www.bkconnection.com/impact.

Dear reader,

Thank you for picking up this book and welcome to the worldwide BK community! You're joining a special group of people who have come together to create positive change in their lives, organizations, and communities.

What's BK all about?

Our mission is to connect people and ideas to create a world that works for all.

Why? Our communities, organizations, and lives get bogged down by old paradigms of self-interest, exclusion, hierarchy, and privilege. But we believe that can change. That's why we seek the leading experts on these challenges—and share their actionable ideas with you.

A welcome gift

To help you get started, we'd like to offer you a **free copy** of one of our bestselling ebooks:

www.bkconnection.com/welcome

When you claim your **free ebook**, you'll also be subscribed to our blog.

Our freshest insights

Access the best new tools and ideas for leaders at all levels on our blog at ideas.bkconnection.com.

Sincerely,

Your friends at Berrett-Koehler